STORYBOOK QUILTING

Storybook QUILTING

Jennifer L. Baker | Laurie E. Mehalko

CHILTON BOOK COMPANY   Radnor, Pennsylvania

Copyright © 1985 by Jennifer L. Baker and Laurie E. Mehalko
All Rights Reserved
Published in Radnor, Pennsylvania 19089, by Chilton Book Company
No part of this book may be reproduced, transmitted or stored
in any form or by any means, electronic or mechanical,
without prior written permission from the publisher
Photography by Jerry Thirion, Thirion Photography, Edwardsville, Illinois
Designed by Arlene Putterman
Manufactured in the United States of America

Library of Congress Cataloging in Publication Data
Baker, Jennifer L.
    Storybook quilting.
    Includes index.
    1. Quilting.   I. Mehalko, Laurie E.   II. Title.
TT835.B26   1985   746.46   84-45699
ISBN 0-8019-7528-X (pbk.)
ISBN 0-8019-7527-1 (hardcover)

1 2 3 4 5 6 7 8 9 0   4 3 2 1 0 9 8 7 6 5

To our children—Andrew, Miriam, and Ross—whose imaginations and love of a good story have inspired our designs.

CONTENTS

ACKNOWLEDGMENTS

To our families, who have endured a lack of our personal attention, quickie meals, and cluttered households. Your supportive tolerance has helped make this book possible.

To Lois Haas, who believed in this project when it was still an idea and cheered enthusiastically as each hurdle was crossed.

Special thanks to Dale Ott for his excellent delivery service, Pam and Dale Ott for offering the seclusion of their home to write, Elayne Mullenix for expert help in sewing, Mary Hochmuth for assistance in marking quilt tops, Ann Allen for professional proofreading, Dixie Morlen for loaning her antique crib, and Kenneth Evers for allowing us to photograph at his home.

To Rosemary Seifried of Highland, IL, and the Zion Lutheran Lydia Sewing Circle of Staunton, IL. Your willingness to interrupt your busy schedules to quilt our quilts has our utmost appreciation.

To our models: Andrew and Miriam Baker, Nikki Duree, Alan Haynes, Katie Heise, Ross Mehalko, Patrick and Stephanie Shen, and Tiffany Spudich. Your patience in posing was greatly appreciated.

To our photographer, Jerry Thirion. Your hard work and concern for detail have added much to this project.

To Kathryn Conover and Lisa Fradkin, our editors, who had confidence in our ability from the start and did their best to make this book a reality.

STORYBOOK QUILTING

Introduction

As mothers of preschoolers, we have done quite a lot of sewing for our own children as well as for the children of friends and relatives. In so doing, we have developed a certain philosophy about children's "things." Sewing for children can be either a wonderful experience or a big headache, depending on your expectations for the finished product. You need to consider the likes and dislikes of the child, the child's parents, and yourself.

What are the child's favorite colors? Does he have a favorite bedtime story? Does she share a room with a younger sibling? Is there a need for two similar but not exactly-the-same outfits?

How do adults view the child? Some see children as miniadults—thus we have designer jeans and high-tech nurseries. Some parents enjoy putting together environments that are fluffy, frilly, and feminine—and also somewhat impractical. Some parents want "the latest" in fashion for their children, while others are big on traditional styles. Finally, some give very little thought to their child's room and clothing. Their philosophy might be expressed as follows: "Kids grow out of their things so quickly, and all they really want to wear are jeans and T-shirts. Their rooms are usually a mess, so why bother?"

If you are not the child's parent, you will also need to consider yourself—at least a little. How do you feel about the item you make being used? Most quilt-makers or seamstresses would like the quilts and clothing they make for children to be used and enjoyed. However, many mothers cannot bring themselves to put the quilt on the bed, where it may get soiled or torn, so they pack it up and store it away until the child is older. One way to encourage its use might be to choose a design with a few large, simple shapes and concentrate on color impact rather than detail in workmanship. Use durable fabrics that will withstand many washings, and try to use machine stitching rather than handwork whenever possible.

Maybe you don't want your quilt to be put on the bed. If so, be sure to add a sleeve on the back for hanging and give instructions on how to hang and care for it. If you think your desires will be at odds with those of the child's parents,

1

try to think of some workable compromises while the quilt is in the planning stages—not after it is done. The same can be said for quilted clothing and accessories, although those items do not usually involve as great an expenditure in terms of time, money, and energy.

At this point, one might well ask, "Are you sure it's worth it? Wouldn't a ready-made dress or bedspread be simpler?" Well, maybe. But we believe that childhood is a special time, full of its own dreams and imaginings. It lasts but a brief moment, and a treasured quilt can heighten a child's awareness of color, shape, and design. It can give warm, comforting feelings of security. It can send messages: "You are important, so important that I wanted to make this special quilt for you." Or: "Your ideas are important—I tried to get some of your favorite things and colors into this quilt." Most of all, a childhood quilt can say "I love you." And it can say it for years to come, when childhood is long past.

That is why we make quilts for our children. We hope you have a similar philosophy and will enjoy making at least one of the projects in this book for a young child you know.

Chapter 1

Quilting Basics

Preparation

ADAPTING COMMERCIAL PATTERNS

Many of the clothing projects in this book call for a commercial pattern as a starting point. When choosing a pattern for a quilted garment, you will want to look for one with no darts, princess lines, or lapels and as few seams as possible. In fact, a basic child's vest pattern can be simplified even further by overlapping the side seams and cutting the front and back as one whole piece (Fig. 1-1). This allows appliqué or quilting designs to continue around the garment without the interruption of side seams.

The garments made to coordinate with a quilted item should be kept fairly simple so that they do not compete with the main attraction. For example, a simple, unadorned dress is usually the best backdrop for a lacy, ruffled pinafore.

SELECTING FABRICS

Specific fabric types have been suggested for particular projects throughout the book, but they are by no means definitive. Especially when sewing for children, you should choose fabrics with regard to the wear and tear they will receive. Sturdier fabrics such as twill, broadcloth, or denim are suitable for vests and jackets that will receive heavy use. Feminine, dainty dresses are prettiest in soft cottons, voiles, and cotton/polyester blends. Whatever fabric you use, you will want it to be washable. This goes for quilts as well as garments and accessories.

Don't forget about lining fabrics. The slick rayon or acetate linings are not appropriate for most children's clothing because they do not wear well and are difficult to work with. Cottons or cotton/polyester blends generally work best. A blend is most serviceable when the lining has little or no quilting. Unless heavily quilted, 100-percent cottons tend to wrinkle when laundered.

Traditionally, many quilts were made with plain linings, but using a coordinating print in a quilt or quilted garment adds a special touch and is more popular today.

Fig. 1-1

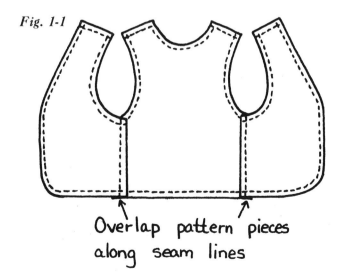

Overlap pattern pieces along seam lines

In most of the instructions, a specific kind of batting is indicated. We prefer the low-loft, higher-density needlepunch batting for most of our garments. This is also referred to as fleece or traditional-weight batting. Regular-loft or even extra-loft batting can be used for the quilts. Whatever you choose to use, make certain that the batting is bonded and washable.

CHOOSING COLOR AND DESIGN

Color choices for children's clothes are limitless. Usually you will want to stick to a particular tone or intensity, such as bright, pastel, or subdued. However, children like many different colors, and even black can be appropriate.

When choosing fabrics for a particular project, you may want to start with a theme fabric that incorporates most of the colors you hope to use. This will make the rest of your fabric selection easier. You may also want to aim for some variety in the size of the print (Fig. 1-2). Small prints alone may be too busy or uninteresting, but a change in scale from small to medium to large can add a touch of excitement and originality. Do not be afraid to use stripes or border prints or to mix different patterns. Experiment with color. Green can be true green, blue-green, or yellow-green. Suggested color choices listed with the projects help clarify the yardage amounts, but they are not the only possibilities.

PREPARING FABRICS, LININGS, AND TRIMS

All fabrics, linings, and trims should be prewashed in warm water with a small amount of detergent before you sew them into a garment or quilt. Prewashing removes sizing and excess color that can cause bleeding or crocking. As a rule, dark and light colors should be washed separately. Fabrics may then be dried in the dryer at the temperature you would use for the completed project.

We cannot overemphasize the importance of prewashing trims, such as prepackaged eyelet, lace, and rickrack, even if the manufacturer guarantees against shrinkage and fading. The time and effort spent putting together a quilt could end in disappointment if these precautions are not followed.

MAKING TEMPLATES

A Template is a pattern piece that may be used several times on a quilt or quilt-related item. Since you often need to trace around them, it is a good idea to make

Fig. 1-2
The combination of different-sized print patterns on the right is much more interesting than the similar-sized patterns on the left.

them out of something sturdier or heavier than paper. Translucent plastic is preferable, but cardboard and sandpaper are also acceptable.

For pieced projects, seam allowances of $\frac{1}{4}''$ may be added to templates. For hand appliqué, add scant $\frac{1}{4}''$ seam allowances to the shape on the fabric after the template has been traced. For machine appliqué, cut the fabric along actual template lines.

All patterns, except for one in the Jack and the Beanstalk chapter, are actual size. (That pattern must be enlarged according to the scale that's given.) The composite drawings provide you with a placement guide for overlapping pattern parts. Trace the outline of the full figure on the background fabric and use it as a placement guide when you are ready to appliqué. To make composite templates from this figure, you must imagine the parts of the design that are not actually visible—in other words, parts that will be underneath other parts, as shown by dotted lines on Figure 1-3—and make the pattern pieces accordingly.

USING SCALED PATTERNS AND DRAWINGS

When you need to enlarge a pattern or position appliqués on background fabric according to a scaled drawing (in the case of the "Fe, Fi, Fo, Fum" quilt in Chapter 7), pay close attention to the scale. Use graph paper or make your own grid on a large piece of paper or newsprint (Fig. 1-4). Use a ruler and a T-square or a 45° triangle to make certain that your graph is square. When your graph is completed, transfer the design square-by-square (Fig. 1-5). Remember that no seam allowances have been added to the pattern pieces. You must do this on your own if you plan to hand appliqué. In the case of the "Fe, Fi, Fo, Fum" quilt in Chapter 7, it is not necessary to enlarge the entire quilt top. Just cut the individual pattern pieces according to specifications and use the scaled drawing to place them on the background fabric.

Another option for enlarging patterns is to use a copier. Slight distortions will occur, but this will not affect the appliqué patterns. A copier *cannot* be used successfully for pieced designs, such as the triangular border on the Red Riding Hood doll quilt in Chapter 4.

Fig. 1-3

Fig. 1-4

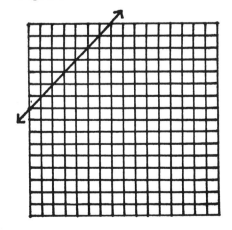

Fig. 1-5

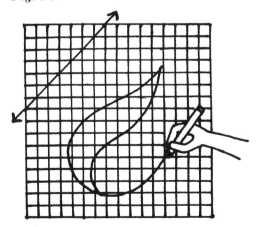

MARKING, FUSING, AND CUTTING

All appliqués and pattern pieces should be placed along the grain of the fabric whenever possible. If there is no arrow on the pattern piece to indicate the direction of the grain, align the grain line of the appliqué with that of the background fabric (Fig. 1-6). If you fail to place appliqués on the straight of grain, puckering may occur when the item is laundered.

Trace around the template with a pencil or water-soluble marker. Yellow, silver, or white architect's pencils (for marking blueprints) work nicely on dark fabrics. Always mark appliqué patterns on the right side of the fabric and pieced patterns on the wrong side. Add a scant $\frac{1}{4}''$ seam allowance to the fabric if you plan to hand appliqué, since none are included on the pattern pieces (Fig. 1-7).

For machine appliqué, we recommend fusing fabric to lightweight interfacing. (Fusible interfacing prevents fraying and puckering of the curved edges when the appliqué edges are satin stitched.)

To simplify the process, begin by tracing the appliqué designs onto the right side of the fabric as you would for hand appliqué (Fig. 1-8A). However, you will not have to leave space for seam allowances. Then turn the fabric over and place the fusible interfacing on the wrong side only under the portion needed (Fig. 1-8B). This eliminates the need to cut out the same piece twice—once from fabric and once from interfacing—and it also conserves fabric and interfacing. Use a

Fig. 1-6

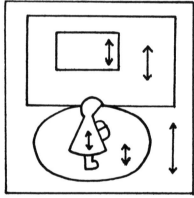

Fig. 1-7

Fig. 1-8

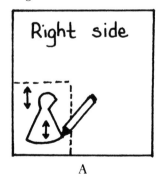

steam iron on the "wool" setting for fusing, holding the iron in one place for ten seconds without shifting or moving it. When the fabric is completely fused, cut out the appliqués.

Note that some projects call for cutting reverse pattern pieces. These will be noted by *r* in the drawings and patterns.

Construction

APPLIQUÉ

Appliqué is the process of applying or "laying down" one fabric on top of another. It can be done by hand or machine. Hand appliqué is generally used to achieve a finer, more delicate look; machine appliqué works well for items that will receive more wear and tear.

By Hand

For accuracy in placement, trace around the individual pattern pieces or transfer the outline of the full figure onto the background fabric (Fig. 1-9). This step is essential for hand appliqué, in which one piece at a time is positioned and stitched down. Without some sort of guide to follow, distortion can easily occur.

Begin by stitching the farthermost piece first. (Follow the sequence in the individual project instructions.) Pin or glue-stick the appliqué in place if necessary and slipstitch with matching thread. Some methods call for basting the appliqué edges before stitching, but we prefer to match the stitching line on the appliqué with the outline on the background fabric and roll the seam allowance under with the needle as we go (Fig. 1-10).

For ease in shaping, clip deep inside curves and corners all the way to the seam line (Fig. 1-10). Whipstitch these areas with tiny, close stitches to secure them. To make sharp points, stitch to the corner (Fig. 1-11A), turn up the end of the point by taking a stitch right at the tip (Fig. 1-11B), and then stitch the other side (Fig. 1-11C).

To appliqué bias strips, pin the bias on the marked seam line, right sides together, overlapping by $\frac{1}{4}''$ (Fig. 1-12). Sew together with small running stitches.

Fig. 1-9

Fig. 1-10

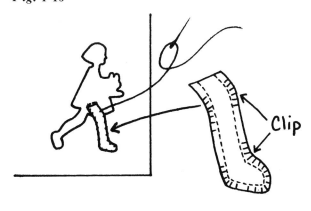

Clip

Fold the bias over the outline of the strip, turning the raw edge under ¼". Slipstitch in place (Fig. 1-13).

When appliqué pieces overlap, do not turn under the edges of the piece covered by the overlapping appliqué. Keep appliqué stitches tight and even for straight seams and smooth curves. When the stitching has been completed, turn the work over and trim the excess background fabric from behind the appliqué, leaving ¼" seam allowances. This reduces the bulk of the fabric and interfacing and makes quilting easier.

By Machine

Machine appliqué is relatively fast, easy, and durable. For ease in stitching, we back most appliqués with fusible interfacing before satin stitching the edges. Once all the appliqués have been cut out, position them on the background fabric in the proper arrangement. (Remember, they have no seam allowances.) Pin or glue-stick them in place and begin satin stitching the edges with a close zigzag stitch. Use matching thread to achieve the neatest results, and keep the outside edge of the stitching just off the edge of the appliqué (Fig. 1-14). We also recommend that you use lightweight nonfusible interfacing behind the background fabric to reduce puckering. Trim the excess after you have completed the satin stitching.

In a few cases, when the pieces to be machine appliquéd are very large, have fairly straight edges, or will need to be quilted through, it is not practical to bond them with fusible interfacing. To machine appliqué these pieces, pin or glue-stick

Fig. 1-11

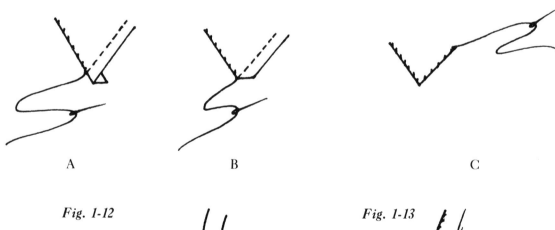

A   B   C

Fig. 1-12   *Fig. 1-13*

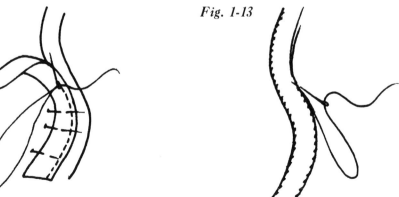

them in place and then stitch around the edges with a wide zigzag stitch. Stitch a second time with a close zigzag or satin stitch (Fig. 1-15).

SHADOW APPLIQUÉ

Shadow appliqué is a method of sandwiching an appliqué insert between a background fabric and a sheer overlay, such as voile or batiste. Fleece can be included under the background fabric to give the project more depth or texture. Small running stitches like those used for quilting hold all the layers together and define the appliqué insert. Quilting is usually done with a thread much darker than the appliqué fabrics or with different colors altogether. When the hand stitching is completed, the project is lined with a lightweight fabric.

Special Supplies

Fusible interfacing: All appliqué inserts are backed with fusible interfacing to add stability and prevent fraying.

Glue stick or spray adhesive: Holds appliqué insert in position on the background fabric under the sheer overlay until quilting has been completed.

Pencils: For tracing patterns onto fabric and marking quilting designs.

Water-soluble marker: For marking quilting designs on sheer overlay fabric.

Choosing the Fabrics

Background fabric: Choose a lightweight to medium-weight white or solid-color fabric. Dark background fabrics are good for light-colored appliqué inserts, while darker appliqué inserts stand out on a light-colored background. Contrast is important.

Appliqué insert: Choose the color according to the color of the background fabric. In general, appliqué inserts should be very light or bright in color. Gray tones

Fig. 1-14   *Fig. 1-15*

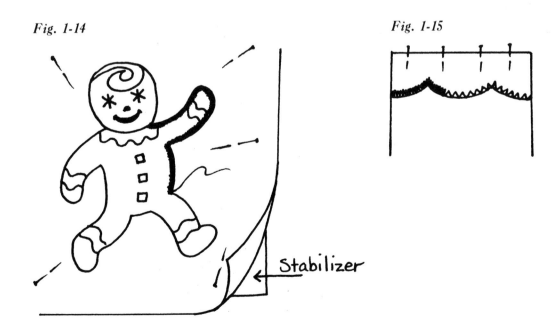

Stabilizer

or dull colors have little visual impact because they usually don't show through the sheer overlay.

Sheer overlay: The sheer overlay fabric is usually a white voile or batiste. Off-white or ecru shades can be used to give a more "antique" look to the project.

Batting: Regular bonded quilt batting can be used, but fleece or needlepunch batting is preferable. Because of its light weight, it is less bulky, which makes it ideal for garments. And because of its density, it can be quilted directly without using a backing fabric. The stitches do not pull out. This is an important consideration, since there are already so many layers to get a needle through.

Lining: Use a lightweight, wrinkle-resistant broadcloth to back the whole project when the quilting is completed.

Cutting and Marking

Always make sure that all fabrics are placed on the straight of the grain. Also, because quilting draws up the fabric, decreasing the finished size of the project, cut the background and overlay fabrics a little larger than you want them. They can always be trimmed to the correct size when quilting is completed.

Quilting the Appliqués

Quilting is done around each appliqué just off the outer edge and on the designated quilting lines shown on the pattern pieces. Quilting through the appliqué inserts is necessary to hold them in place and keep the edges from shifting or curling in laundering.

PIECING

Piecing is the term used to describe the sewing together of small pieces of fabric to make a new design or pattern. It may be done by hand or machine. Pin pieces with right sides together and match the corners (Fig. 1-16). Stitch from corner to corner, starting and stopping with two backstitches $\frac{1}{4}''$ from the edge of the fabric. Do not sew down seam allowances. Press seams to one side. Continue in the same manner as you join more pieces together, always being careful to keep seam allowances free. The seam allowances may be sewn down as the borders are attached to the pieced area.

EMBROIDERY STITCHES

Many of the projects in this book call for a small amount of embroidery work for details on the appliqués. The stitches used are shown in Figures 1-17, 1-18, and

Fig. 1-16

Fig. 1-17

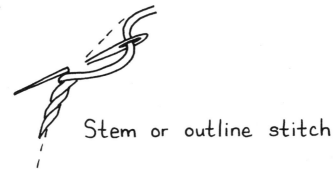

Stem or outline stitch

Fig. 1-18

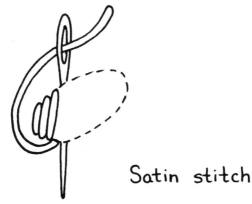

Satin stitch

Fig. 1-19

French knot

1-19. For embroidery work, use perle cotton or six-strand embroidery floss, which is usually divided into three strands.

MAKING A CONTINUOUS BIAS

The following is a simple method of making bias for binding seams and edges. Make a perfect square of fabric by folding one corner down on itself diagonally (Fig. 1-20). Press the diagonal crease and cut along the vertical and horizontal edges of the folded triangle. Unfold the square and cut on the diagonal line to form two equal triangles (Fig. 1-21). With right sides together, sew the triangles together along a straight-grain edge with a $\frac{1}{4}''$ seam allowance (Fig. 1-22). Press the seam open. Mark lines the desired width apart, usually $1\frac{1}{4}''$, on the wrong side of the fabric (Fig. 1-23). Bring opposite sides together, matching pencil lines, offsetting by a one-strip width (Fig. 1-24). Stitch with $\frac{1}{4}''$ seam allowance. Press the seam open. Cut along pencil lines for one continuous strip. You will essentially be cutting out a spiral.

Fig. 1-20

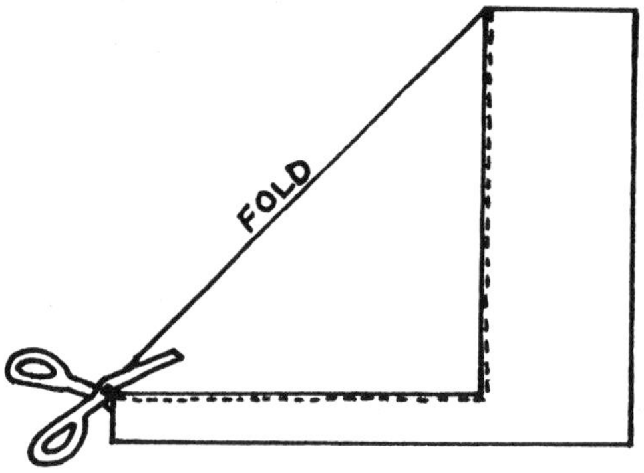

Fig. 1-21

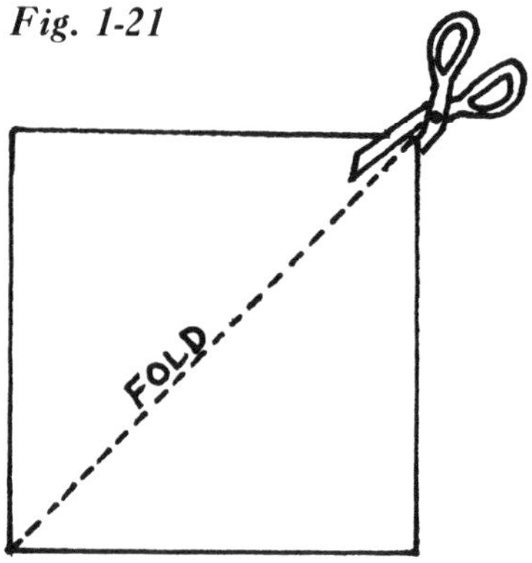

Fig. 1-22

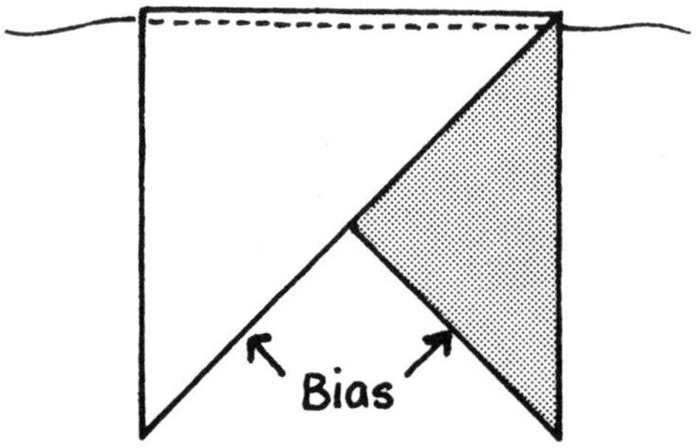

Fig. 1-23

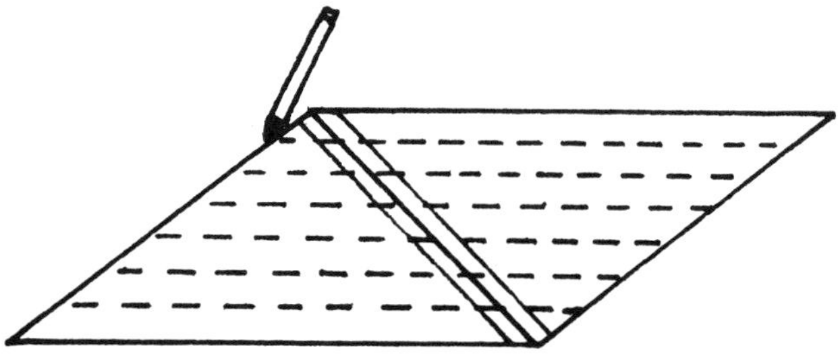

Fig. 1-24

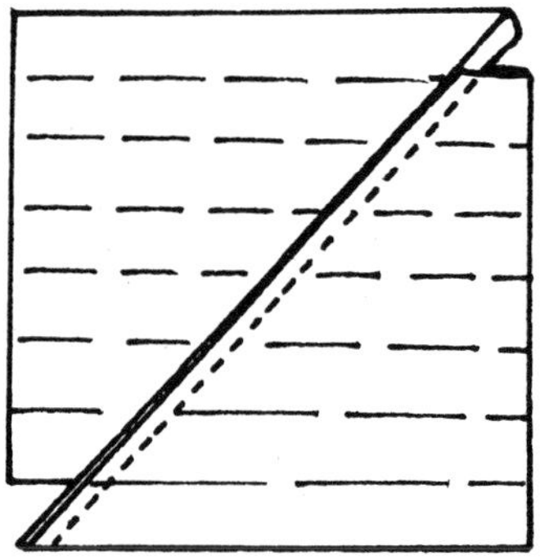

Finishing Touches

BUTTON LOOPS

When a vest or jacket meets in front but does not overlap, it may be necessary to make some sort of button loops to hold the garment together. To make button loops, cut a strip of fabric on the straight of the grain 1″ wide and 2½″ long for every loop you will need. For instance, four loops could be made from a strip measuring 1″ × 10″. Press the strip in half lengthwise, wrong sides together. Unfold and press both raw edges to center. Fold the strip in half and topstitch the folded edges closed (Fig. 1-25A). Cut loops to the desired length, then fold and stitch (Fig. 1-25B). You may also leave the loop unstitched to create a softer, less-tailored effect. With raw edges matching, sew the loops to the jacket or vest front. When the lining or binding is attached, the loops will be facing the right direction.

BUTTONS

Give some thought to choosing just the right buttons for your special quilted garment. A button can merely hold the garment together, or it can provide that perfect finishing touch. For instance, wooden buttons resembling beans were used on the Jack and the Beanstalk vest, while lustrous, pearllike buttons were used for the Sleeping Beauty vest. When you have given so much thought and effort to a garment, don't skimp on the buttons. Make them "do something" for the garment.

MITERED CORNERS

For Borders

When mitered corners are called for in a border treatment, you must allow some extra length on the border strip. Center the strip on the block, pin, and stitch out from the center to each corner (Fig. 1-26). Stop stitching ¼″ from the edge of the fabric. Press strip at a 45° angle (Fig. 1-27). Stitch corners together along the pressed line (Fig. 1-28). Trim seam to ¼″ and press again.

Fig. 1-25

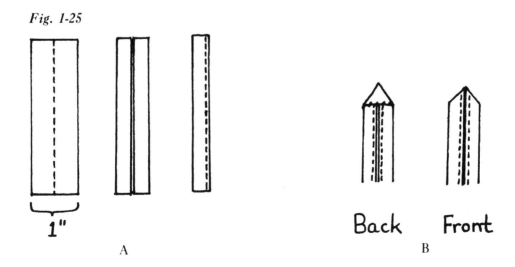

1″

A   Back   Front   B

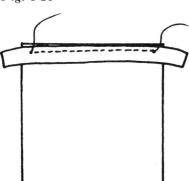

Fig. 1-26

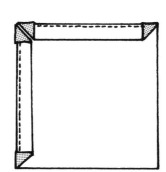

Fig. 1-27

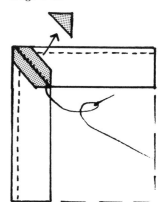

Fig. 1-28

For Bindings

If a quilt or wallhanging has mitered corners, it is appropriate to miter the binding corners as well. This can be done in several different ways:

Self-binding—Use this method when you are binding with the backing (lining fabric) or with straight-grain strips. For straight-grain binding, begin by stitching strips to the top of the quilt, right sides together, just as you did for mitered borders (see Fig. 1-26). Continue making mitered corners with the strips as shown in Figures 1-27 and 1-28. Then, for straight-grain binding or binding with the backing, fold in the tip of the outer corner so that it touches the intersecting seam lines (Fig. 1-29). Trim out a small triangle of the folded corner to reduce bulk (Fig. 1-30). Next, fold in the edges of the binding so that a perfect miter is formed (Fig. 1-31). Pin and stitch in place.

Continuous-bias binding—With right sides together, stitch the binding to the quilted edge, stopping $\frac{1}{4}''$ from the corner (Fig. 1-32). Fold the binding back on itself, then align it with the next edge (Fig. 1-33). Begin stitching at the top of the raw edge and sew through all layers (Fig. 1-34). Turn the binding to the lining side, and you will have a miter at the corner (Fig. 1-35). Repeat with the other corners. Secure the mitered fold with a few stitches, turn the raw edge of the binding under $\frac{1}{4}''$, and slipstitch it to the quilt.

Binding with a double-mitered corner—With right sides together, stitch the binding strips to the quilt or garment, stopping $\frac{1}{4}''$ from the corner. Pull the strip extensions out from where they meet at the corners and align the ends with right sides together (Fig. 1-36). Be sure to keep the quilt or the garment out of the way when you do this. Beginning exactly at the corner point where your two stitching lines intersect, start stitching out on the binding at a 45° angle. (It may help to mark this seam line in advance.) Using 15 to 20 stitches per inch, sew to the midpoint of the binding strip. Pivot and sew back to the opposite side at a 90° angle. Stop $\frac{1}{4}''$ from the edge (Fig. 1-37). Trim the excess binding to $\frac{1}{4}''$ from the seam line (Fig. 1-38A). Push out the mitered point with a pin or pencil if necessary. Pull the binding over the corner to the back side, turning under the $\frac{1}{4}''$ seam allowance. Pin in place and slipstitch to the back of the garment or quilt (Fig. 1-38B).

Fig. 1-29

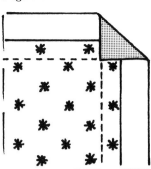

Fig. 1-30

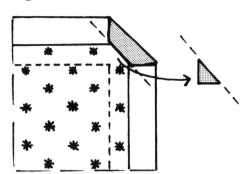

Fig. 1-31

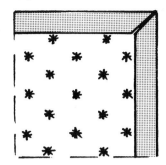

Fig. 1-32

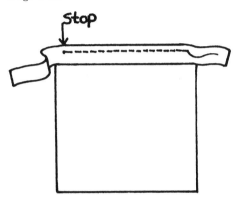

Fig. 1-33

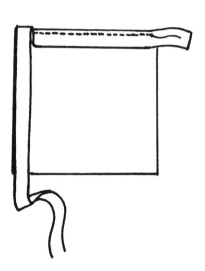

Fig. 1-34

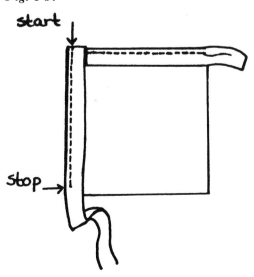

Fig. 1-35

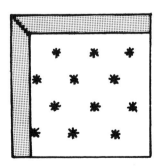

Fig. 1-36

Fig. 1-37

Fig. 1-38

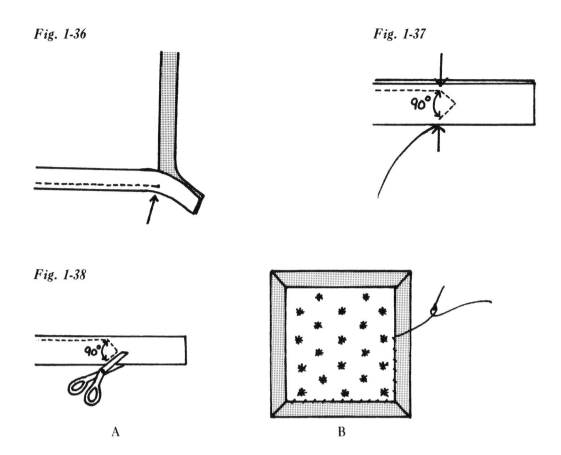

A   B

MARKING QUILTING LINES

The item to be quilted should be pressed carefully, laid on a flat surface, and then marked with quilting lines. Some items have to be marked after they are basted together with batting and lining. In these instances, stretch the project in a quilting hoop for marking, or smooth it out as evenly as possible on a flat surface.

Use a pencil or water-soluble marker for marking. If you use a water-soluble marker, be sure to wash the garment or quilt thoroughly after quilting. This will prevent the marks from reappearing later. To mark dark fabrics, use a white, yellow, or silver architect's pencil, available in office-supply stores. Whether you use a pencil or a marker, remember to mark lightly and only where necessary.

BASTING THE QUILT TOP, BATTING, AND LINING

The quilt top must be basted together with the batting and lining before you can begin to quilt. Begin by preparing the lining fabric for the back of the quilt. If you are making a quilt larger than crib size, the backing will probably need to be seamed. Divide the distance in half and center the seam so that both sides of the backing are the same size. Press the seam open. Some quilters eliminate this piecing step by using a sheet to back the quilt, but this is usually not a good idea because most sheets have a high thread count and are difficult to quilt through. If the seamed backing bothers you, use a print fabric for the lining and the seam will be less noticeable.

Fig. 1-39

19
*Quilting
Basics*

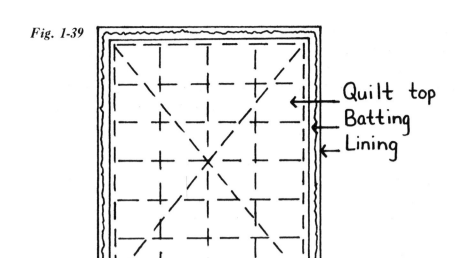

Quilt top
Batting
Lining

Lay the quilt lining or backing wrong side up on a flat surface. Lay the quilt batting over the lining fabric and smooth out any bumps or bulges with your hands. Top the batting with the freshly pressed quilt top. The batting and lining fabric should extend at least 1″ or 2″ beyond the quilt top all the way around. Beginning at the middle of the quilt, stitch out from the center vertically, horizontally, and diagonally with large basting stitches (Fig. 1-39). Add additional rows of vertical and horizontal basting stitches approximately 5″ to 6″ apart as needed. If you are basting the quilt on a table, remember to baste only the portion lying on top of the table. Check the back of the quilt every now and then to make sure that the lining fabric isn't puckering or wrinkling. Once you begin to quilt, remove the basting stitches as you go along, being careful not to quilt through any of them.

QUILTING

Quilting refers to the small, even stitches that hold the layers of the garment or quilt together. The stitching keeps the multiple layers from shifting and adds to the durability of the garment or quilt. However, what we think about most often when we consider quilting is the beauty and design it adds to an item. Rows of small, even stitches give texture and depth to an otherwise flat piece of fabric, and they define or enhance appliqué and patchwork.

Suggested quilting lines are given for every quilted item in this book. However, if you have an idea for your own quilting design, feel free to experiment. Try to let the design of the project suggest possible quilting lines in order to work for a feeling of unity. Also remember that geometric designs are usually enhanced by curvilinear quilting, while curved appliqué work is enhanced most by straight-line quilting.

Quilting is the finishing touch for your garment, quilt, or accessory. If it is planned carefully and executed correctly, it will add to the overall statement and impact of the project.

Thread

Quilting thread is available in a wide variety of colors, but it is still not possible to get every shade necessary for some projects. When quilting thread cannot be obtained in the correct color, use regular sewing thread coated with beeswax to reduce knotting. (Beeswax is available in most fabric stores.) Because knotting may still occur with quilting thread, you may want to coat this with beeswax as well.

When machine quilting, use regular sewing thread on top and in the bobbin. Try two different colors—one to match the top and one to match the lining. If you balance the tension correctly, neither color should show on the opposite side.

Needles

For hand quilting, use the needles called "betweens." Number 7 or 8 is a typical size to start with if you are a beginning quilter. For machine quilting, use a number 11 ballpoint needle.

Hand Quilting

When you have threaded your needle with a 12″ to 18″ length of thread, make a single knot at the end of the strand. Place the needle through the quilt top a half inch or so from where you wish to begin quilting. Bring the needle up at the starting point and "pop" the knot through the fabric into the batting (Fig. 1-40). Make a small backstitch to anchor the knot, then proceed to quilt with small, even running stitches. When you have finished quilting, make a single knot and pull it to the top of the quilt with your needle (Fig. 1-41). "Pop" the knot into the batting, come up with the needle half an inch away, and clip the thread at the surface of the quilt (Fig. 1-42).

Machine Quilting

Machine quilting is usually most successful on vertical, horizontal, or diagonal lines. Machine quilting curved lines will frequently cause the lining fabric to pucker or pull. If an even-feed attachment is available for your sewing machine, you may wish to use it for machine quilting.

Fig. 1-40

Fig. 1-41

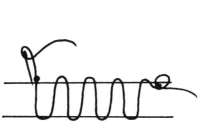

Fig. 1-42

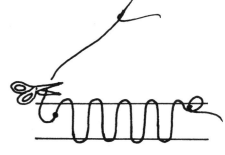

TYING

Some projects call for tying instead of quilting. For this you may use yarn, perle cotton, six-strand embroidery floss, or even narrow ribbon. Baste the quilt together with the batting and lining as you would if you had planned to quilt it. Mark the pattern for tying with a pencil, straight pins, or safety pins. With the quilt right side up, run the tying thread or yarn down and up through all layers, taking about a $\frac{1}{8}''$ bite. Clip the threads, leaving them an inch or so long, and tie them with square knots (Fig. 1-43). Trim all ties to a uniform length when stitching is complete.

The general instructions presented in this chapter for preparing fabrics, making templates, marking, fusing, and cutting should be followed for each project in the book.

Fig. 1-43

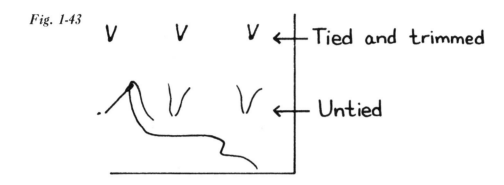

Chapter 2

ansel and Gretel

Fig. 2-1
Crib quilt.

Fig. 2-2
Brother and sister vests.

Fig. 2-3
Rocking-chair cushion.

The quilt, vest, and other related items in this chapter were created in Christmas colors of red, green, and white. (See color section of the book.) If you want a less seasonal look, simply change the bright green to forest green and the red to rust or cranberry. We have done it both ways and have found that subdued colors tend to give a more "antique" look.

Crib Quilt

This Hansel and Gretel storybook quilt is sure to awaken fond childhood memories in the hearts of grown-ups and older children alike. Generations of children have fallen in love with this story. What better way to pass along the pleasures of a childhood classic than in the form of a quilt!

The quilt is assembled in two parts. The center design, which finishes at 20″ × 30″, is machine appliquéd first, with a thin layer of fleece as the batting. The appliquéd scene is then centered over a solid 41″ × 51″ top and hand appliquéd. A high-loft batting is used between the crib-size top and its lining, creating the density needed to show off the fine hand-quilted leaves. See the color section for a photograph of the quilt.

The finished quilt measures 38″ × 48″ inside the ruffled border. Once baby has outgrown this crib quilt, it can be used as a wallhanging or lap quilt for small children.

REQUIREMENTS
Yardage (44″ or 45″ fabric):

> Green solid—$2\frac{2}{3}$ yds. (quilt top, center background, and ruffle)
> Red print—$2\frac{2}{3}$ yds. (center foreground, lining, and ruffle)
> Tan solid—$\frac{1}{2}$ yd. or 16″ × 21″ rectangle (path)
> Dark-brown pindot—1 yd. (trees and border strips)
> Assorted fabric and lace scraps (house details and children)
> High-loft quilt batting—45″ × 60″ rectangle
> Fleece—22″ × 32″ rectangle
> Lightweight nonfusible interfacing (stabilizer)—22″ × 32″ rectangle
> Fusible interfacing—1 yd. (appliqué backing)

Gathered eyelet—$5\frac{1}{2}$ yds. (trim on house and ruffle)
Red and green quilting thread
Matching colored thread for appliqué and sewing

DIRECTIONS

1. Follow the cutting diagrams (Figs. 2-4 and 2-5) for the large quilt areas and ruffle sections.
2. From the dark-brown pindot, cut the border strips (Fig. 2-6). Fuse the remaining pindot and cut out the tree shapes.
3. Fuse the fabrics for the path and house details. (Scrap fabrics used for appliquéing Hansel and Gretel should not be fused because these figures will be hand appliquéd.) Cut out the house, the path, and Hansel and Gretel

from patterns at the end of the chapter. Remember to add a scant $\frac{1}{4}''$ seam allowance to Hansel and Gretel and possibly the gingerbread man (see step 7) for hand appliqué.

4. Start assembling the center design by placing the green background on top of the fleece and stabilizer. Baste around edges to secure (Fig. 2-7).

5. Cut a strip of fusible interfacing $1'' \times 22''$. Fuse it to the back of the 22" top edge of the red-print foreground. Trim the fused edge to form a wavy horizon line. Pin foreground in place, overlapping the green background. Make sure that the lower and side edges are even with the fleece layer. Tack down the

Fig. 2-4

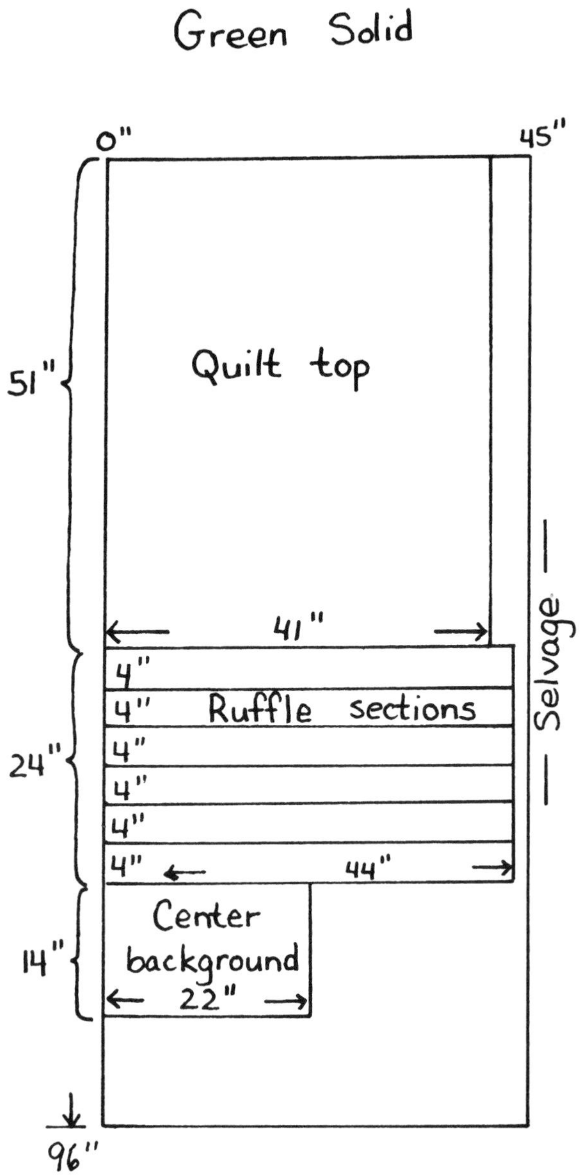

Green Solid

Fig. 2-5

Red Print

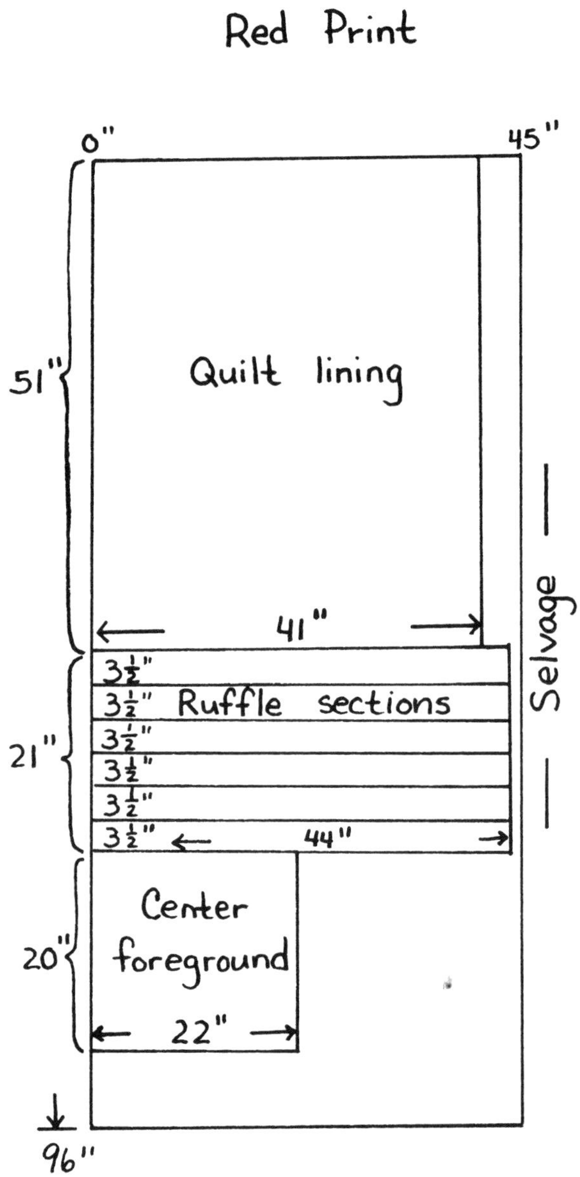

edge of the horizon with glue stick, then machine appliqué through all thicknesses (Fig. 2-8).

6. To position the path, center the house along the horizon and allow the path to lead up to the door (Fig. 2-9A). Set the house aside while you glue and appliqué the path in place. To appliqué the curved path without stretching the curves, first straight stitch the path edges to the background fabric $\frac{1}{16}''$

Fig. 2-6

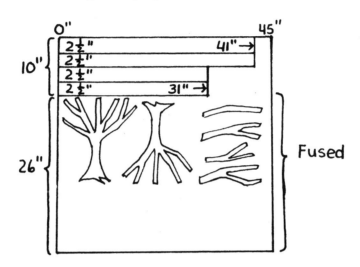

Dark-Brown Pindot

Fig. 2-7

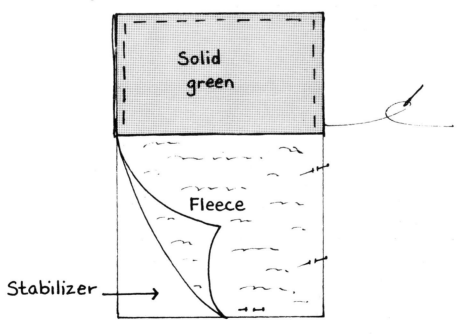

from the edge. Then stitch over the straight stitching with a fine machine satin stitch. You will be pleased with the results—with how flat it lies.

7. Glue and appliqué the trees. Assemble the house parts and glue all pieces in place (Fig. 2-9B). Hand or machine appliqué the gingerbread man on the door before gluing the door in place. Appliqué each piece, leaving the top

Fig. 2-8

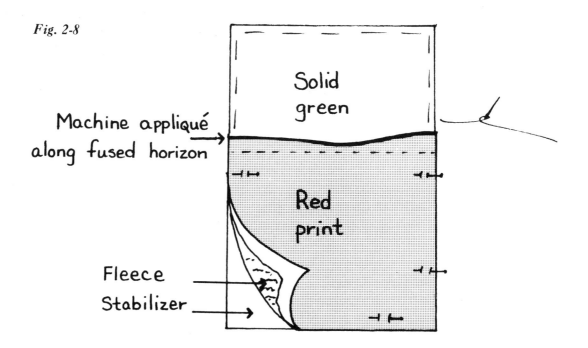

Machine appliqué along fused horizon

Solid green

Red print

Fleece Stabilizer

Fig. 2-9

A

B

edge of the roof open in order to insert the chimney and lace edge (Fig. 2-9). When the chimney and lace edge are sewn, complete the satin stitching on the rooftop. Straight stitch the eyelet and lace trims in place around the roof and door (Fig. 2-10).

8. On the wrong side, trim away the stabilizer from the appliqués.

9. Hand appliqué Hansel and Gretel along the path (see Figure 2-16 for placement). Embroider details on their faces, Hansel's hand, and the path (Fig. 2-11). Use French knots for the eyes, outline stitches for the noses and mouths, and satin stitches for the bread crumbs.

10. Press the completed appliqué scene. Using a ruler or a T-square, true the outside edges by lightly marking seam lines to form a rectangle 20″ × 30″. Double-check to make sure that the corners are square and that you have formed a perfect rectangle. Mark the midpoints of each side with a pencil. The appliquéd scene is now ready to position on the solid quilt top.

11. Fold the solid quilt top (41″ × 51″) in quarters and mark the center point with a pencil. Fold the appliquéd scene in quarters and mark the center with a pin or chalk pencil. Position the appliquéd scene over the quilt top, matching the center points and keeping the outside edges parallel. Hand baste in place, keeping all layers smooth and free of wrinkles.

12. Press under ½″ along the lengths of each border strip. On the right side, strips should be 1½″ wide. Mark the midpoint of each length with a chalk pencil. Right sides up, place the border strips over the raw edges of the center scene, aligning the inside folded edge of each strip with the marked seam lines and matching the midpoints of strips and seams (Fig. 2-12). Pin to secure. Slip-stitch the vertical strips in place first, beginning with the inside edges; then sew the outside edges. Repeat this process for the horizontal strips. The vertical and horizontal strips intersect at corners and extend 3″ into the outside border edge. Slipstitch the short ends to the quilt top, tucking under the seam allowance (Fig. 2-13).

13. Turn the quilt top to the wrong side and cut out the solid-green layer of fabric

Fig. 2-10

Straight stitch eyelet and trims

Fig. 2-11

Fig. 2-12

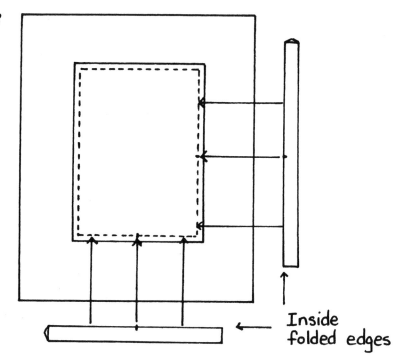

Inside
folded edges

Fig. 2-13

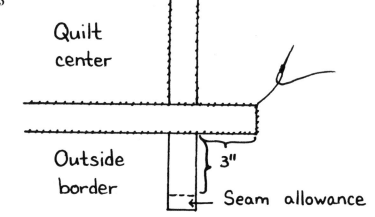

Quilt
center

Outside
border

3"

Seam allowance

behind the appliquéd rectangle. Trim to within ½" of the slipstitching (Fig. 2-14). This will make hand quilting easier by eliminating a layer of fabric.

14. Carefully press the entire quilt top on the right side. To true the entire quilt top as you did the center rectangle, spread out the top and mark the outer-edge seam lines 7½" from the border strips on all sides. The area formed should measure 38" × 48". There should be a 1" seam allowance outside the rectangle.

15. Ruffle: End to end, right sides together, join the print ruffle sections with a ½" seam to form a long, continuous loop. Along one length, press under ¼" and under again ¼". Stitch along the folded edge to form a ¼" hem.

16. Repeat for the solid ruffle sections.

17. With raw edges even and right sides up, pin the print loop on top of the solid loop. Machine stitch two rows of gathering stitches ½" and ⅜" from the raw edge around the double loop.

18. Before gathering the ruffle, mark the loop in eight equal sections. Mark the perimeter of the quilt top in eight equal sections. Gather up one ruffle section at a time to fit each quilt section. This will give you even gathering all the way around. Pin the ruffle to the quilt top right sides together, raw edges outward, but not even. The ruffle has a $\frac{1}{2}''$ seam allowance. Therefore, lay the ruffle over the marked seam line with $\frac{1}{2}''$ of the raw edge extended into the 1″ quilt seam allowance. Stitch the ruffle to the quilt top along the marked seam line.

19. With the right side of the quilt facing up, iron the ruffle flat toward the center of the quilt.

Fig. 2-14

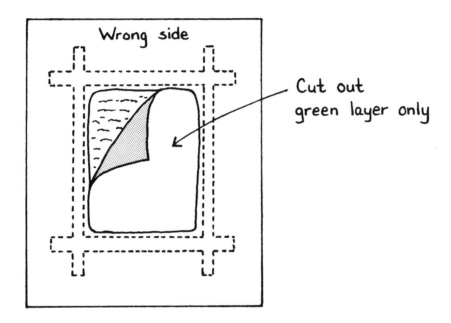

Fig. 2-15

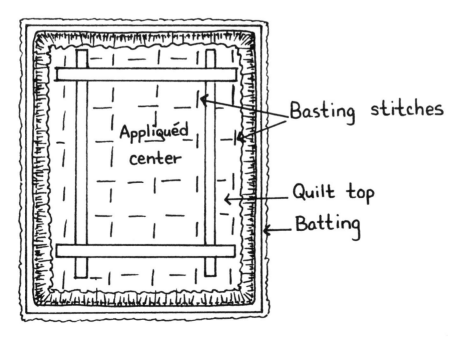

20. Spread open the high-loft quilt batting and place the quilt top over the batting right side up, ruffle inward. Hand baste the quilt top to the batting (Fig. 2-15).

21. Spread the quilt lining right side up on a flat surface. Position the basted top over the quilt lining right side down, ruffle inward. Smooth out the top, matching the raw edges of the quilt top and lining. Pin to secure. Sew together along the stitching line that attached the ruffle, leaving a 12″ opening on one side to turn. Stitch a second seam close to the first for additional reinforcement. Trim the seam allowance and corners. Trim away the batting from the seam allowance. Turn the quilt right side out. Smooth out the quilt, remove the basting, and press lightly along the turned edges.

Fig. 2-16
Leaf groupings and quilting lines on crib quilt.

22. Slipstitch the opening closed. Run long basting stitches through all thicknesses along the center of the border strips and other areas of the quilt to secure the layers for quilting.

23. Using a pencil or water-soluble marker, trace the leaf pattern onto the center background around the tree limbs and around the outside border. Overlap some of the leaves in interesting groupings for a more natural look (Fig. 2-16).

24. Hand quilt in the seam line along both edges of the border strips, along the path and horizon, and around the tree trunks and house. Mark and quilt the center foreground in a pattern that echoes the path (Fig. 2-16). Finally, quilt all traced leaf motifs.

25. On the right side, machine stitch the gathered eyelet around the quilt, sewing through the ruffles close to the quilted edge.

Brother and Sister Vests

This brother-and-sister combination will add a touch of whimsy to any formal occasion, especially around the Christmas holidays. The vests combine machine appliqué for durability and hand quilting for that personal touch that makes a child feel special. See the color section of the book for photographs of the front and back of the vests.

REQUIREMENTS FOR EACH VEST

Commercial vest pattern in child's size—one back and one front piece; no darts, princess lines, or lapels

Yardage for each vest (44″ fabric):

Green solid—$\frac{1}{2}$ to $\frac{3}{4}$ yd. (check pattern requirements)

Red print—1 yd. (foreground and lining)

Brown pindot—$\frac{1}{2}$ yd. (trees)

Assorted fabric scraps (remaining appliqués)

Fleece—$\frac{1}{2}$ to $\frac{3}{4}$ yd.

Lightweight nonfusible interfacing (stabilizer)—$\frac{1}{2}$ to $\frac{3}{4}$ yd.

Lightweight fusible interfacing—$\frac{3}{4}$ yd.

Two buttons

Green quilting thread

Coordinated thread for appliqué and sewing

Additional requirements for girl's vest:

White eyelet trim, $\frac{1}{2}$″ wide—$\frac{2}{3}$ yd. (roof)

White lace trim, $\frac{1}{4}$″ wide—$\frac{1}{4}$ yd. (house)

Note: No yardages are given for girl's dirndl skirt. Follow commercial pattern yardage charts for the desired size.

DIRECTIONS

1. Adapt the commercial pattern according to the instructions in Chapter 1, and cut out all pieces needed to construct the vest.

2. Spread out and pin together, from bottom to top, the lining, nonfusible

interfacing, fleece, and green fabric. Pin the vest pattern in place and cut through all thicknesses. Remove the vest lining and set aside. Hand baste the remaining layers together around outside edges.

3. Fuse and cut fabrics for the paths, trees, and house. For the boy's vest, fuse and cut fabrics for the owl and woodpile. All hand-appliquéd pieces (Hansel and Gretel and the ax on the boy's vest; the mushrooms on the girl's vest) are given a scant $\frac{1}{4}''$ seam allowance before cutting and they are not fused.

4. To make the foreground, fuse a strip of red-print fabric 6″ wide and 36″ long. Fold the strip in half crosswise and pin. Mark a wavy line along the top for the horizon and cut off the top edge (Fig. 2-17).

5. Using a glue stick or pins, position the foreground in place and machine appliqué along the horizon through all thicknesses. Trim the bottom and side edges even so that they match the vest. Cut away the green fabric from underneath the foreground to make later appliquéing easier.

6. Position the paths, glue to secure, and machine appliqué in place (Fig. 2-18).

7. Appliqué the remaining pieces in the following order:
   Boy's vest—House, owl, trees, and woodpile (Fig. 2-19). Hand appliqué Hansel, Gretel, and the ax.
   Girl's vest—Trees and house (Fig. 2-20). Hand appliqué the mushrooms.
   (For detailed instructions on appliquéing the house on the girl's vest, see step 7 in the Hansel and Gretel quilt instructions.) Straight stitch the eyelet and lace trims in place around the roof, chimney, and door.

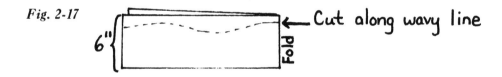

Fig. 2-17

6″ { Fold

Cut along wavy line

Fig. 2-18
Boy's vest—appliqué paths first.

Fig. 2-19
Woodpile—assemble pile by number. Then stitch around edges of assembled pile.

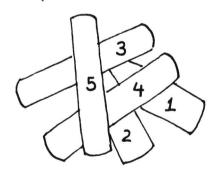

8. Trim away the stabilizer from the wrong side of the vest.

9. On the boy's vest, embroider details on the children, owl, and path (see Fig. 2-11 and step 9 of the quilt instructions).

10. With right sides together, sew the lining to the vest, leaving the shoulder seams open. Trim seams and clip curves. Turn to the right side and press (Fig. 2-21).

11. With right sides together, join the shoulder seams by hand using small stitches. On the inside, slipstitch the lining at the shoulder seams.

12. On the right side, trace the leaf pattern onto the background in random groupings along tree limbs (Fig. 2-22). Hand quilt the leaf outlines through all layers, including the lining. Quilt along the horizon line and around the houses to secure the lining.

13. Make buttonholes and sew on buttons to finish.

Fig. 2-20
Girl's vest.

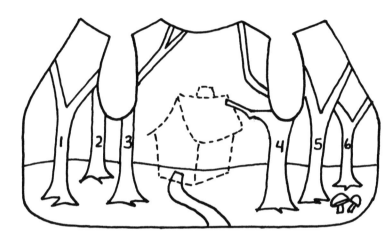

Fig. 2-21

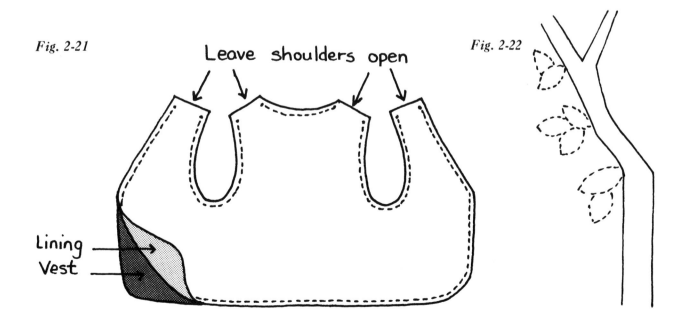

Leave shoulders open

Lining

Vest

Fig. 2-22

Rocking-Chair Cushions

These Hansel and Gretel rocking-chair cushions (see color section for photograph) could be a striking focal point in a little girl's bedroom and a treasured place for her to sit curled up with her favorite storybook friends. It could also add a decorative touch to a grandma's living room when family and friends are gathered for the holidays.

The finished size of the back cushion is $15\frac{1}{2}'' \times 20''$, the seat cushion $13'' \times 15\frac{1}{2}''$, but the instructions tell you how to make cushions that will fit your rocking chair exactly.

REQUIREMENTS

Yardage (44" fabric):

> Green solid—1 yd. (chair back and seat, ruffles, ties)
> Red print—1 yd. (back and seat lining, foreground, ruffles, ties)
> Tan solid—9" × 9" square (path)
> Assorted fabric scraps and lace (house and trees)
> Fleece or polyester batting—20" × 36" rectangle
> Lightweight fusible interfacing—$\frac{1}{2}$ yd.
> Lightweight nonfusible interfacing (stabilizer)—$12\frac{1}{2}'' \times 19''$ rectangle
> Gathered eyelet trim—3 yds. (roof, ruffled edges of chair back and seat)

Green quilting thread

Coordinated thread for appliqué and sewing

DIRECTIONS

1. Make a paper pattern for the rocking-chair cushions, following the layout in Figure 2-23. A seam allowance of $\frac{5}{8}''$ is already included on all sides. From the green solid, cut one chair back, one chair seat, two 4" × 45" ruffles, one 4" × 35" ruffle, two $1\frac{1}{4}'' \times 20''$ ties, and two $1\frac{1}{4}'' \times 26''$ ties. From the red print, cut one chair back (lining), one seat (lining), one foreground (fused), two $3\frac{1}{2}'' \times 45''$ ruffles, one $3\frac{1}{2}'' \times 35''$ ruffle, and two $1\frac{1}{4}'' \times 20''$ ties. If your rocking chair is a different size, measure the length and width of the back and the width and depth of the seat, and adjust the pattern accordingly. Be sure to allow for seam allowances. Follow the same basic shape as that shown in Figure 2-23. Mark a curved horizon line approximately 9" from the lower edge of the chair back. Trace the lower section onto another piece of paper for the foreground (Fig. 2-23).

2. From the nonfusible interfacing, cut one chair back. From the fleece, cut one back and two seats.

3. For the chair back, baste together around the edges of the solid green, the fleece, and the nonfusible stabilizer. Machine appliqué the horizon, path, trees, and house as for the quilt and vests (see steps 5, 6, and 7 of the quilt instructions). Trim away the stabilizer from the wrong side after completing all appliqué work.

4. For the chair seat, baste together around the edges the solid green and two

layers of fleece. Two layers of fleece are used in the seat for additional padding and comfort.

5. Ruffles: You will need a double ruffle (one solid, one print) that is 78″ long for the chair back and another that is 45″ long for the chair seat. Prepare as for the quilt, except note that the ruffle goes around only three sides of each pad. Therefore, hem the short ends of the ruffles before hemming the lengths (Fig. 2-24).

Fig. 2-23

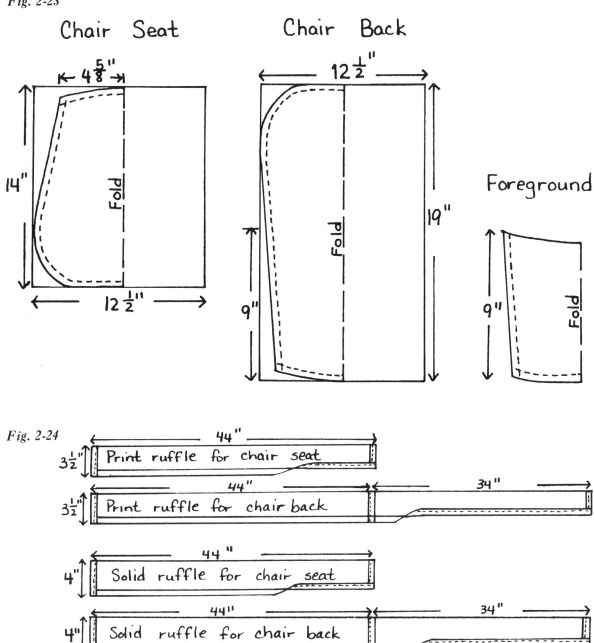

Fig. 2-24

6. Ties: There are two different ways of making the ties. Use the one that works best for you. (*A*) Right sides together, fold each tie section in half lengthwise. Sew a ¼″ seam along the raw edges, leaving one end open to turn. You will probably need a loop turner or small safety pin to turn the tie right side out. Slipstitch the opening closed. Or (*B*) fold each lengthwise edge in toward the center and fold it again lengthwise. Tuck the short ends to the inside and edgestitch close to the outside folded edges (Fig. 2-25).

Fig. 2-25

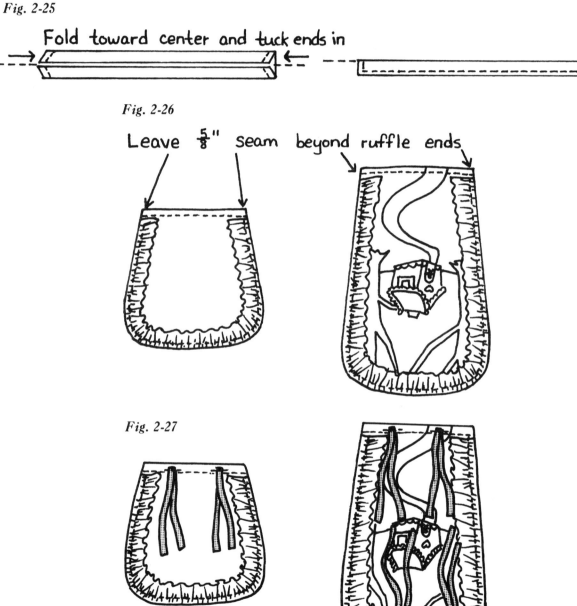

Fold toward center and tuck ends in

Fig. 2-26

Leave ⅝″ seam beyond ruffle ends

Fig. 2-27

7. With right sides together, raw edges even, pin the gathered ruffles to the seat and back cushions, leaving a $\frac{5}{8}''$ seam to extend beyond the ruffle ends (Fig. 2-26). Stitch the ruffles to the cushions, taking a $\frac{5}{8}''$ seam.

8. Fold the ties in half and tack them to the chair cushions inside the seam allowances (Fig. 2-27). Note that the folded middle of the ties is toward the outside raw edges of the cushion and that the loose ends are toward the center of the cushion. Sew the 20″ red pair to the bottom of the chair back, the 26″ green pair to the top of the chair back, and the 20″ green pair to the back of the chair seat.

9. With right sides together, sew the linings to the chair cushions, leaving the straight sides open for turning. (See step 21 from the quilt instructions.)

10. Follow steps 23 to 25 of the quilt instructions for quilting and finishing. Hand quilting should be limited to the leaf motifs, since this is the only quilting that will really show up because of the thin batting.

Photograph Album Cover

The Hansel and Gretel album cover (see color section for photograph) makes a great gift for that special someone on your Christmas list, and it is quick and easy. The cover is done almost entirely by machine with a minimum of hand quilting. It would make a delightful cover for a child's scrapbook or prized photo album documenting those precious growing years.

The finished size of the album cover is $12\frac{1}{2}'' \times 13'' \times 2\frac{1}{2}''$. Yardages are based on a closed 50-page photo album.

REQUIREMENTS

Yardage (44″ fabric):
   Green solid—$\frac{1}{2}$ yd. (cover)
   Red print—$\frac{2}{3}$ yd. (lining, facings, foreground)
   Assorted fabric and lace scraps for appliqués
   Gathered eyelet trim—$\frac{2}{3}$ yd. (roof)
   Fleece—$\frac{1}{2}$ yd.
   Lightweight nonfusible interfacing (stabilizer)—14″ × 30″ rectangle
   Lightweight fusible interfacing—$\frac{1}{2}$ yd.
Green quilting thread
Coordinated thread for appliqué and sewing

DIRECTIONS

1. For any size album, lay the album open and measure its height and total width from front edge to back edge (Fig. 2-28). Add $\frac{3}{4}''$ seam allowance to all sides of the album cover and front- and back-cover facings.

2. From the green solid, cut the album cover (Fig. 2-29). From the red print, cut the album-cover lining (Fig. 2-29) and two facings for the front and back covers (Fig. 2-30).

3. For the foreground, fuse to interfacing a length of red print and cut a rectangle measuring 6″ × 30″. Fuse the two pieces. Trim the top edge to form the horizon. (See step 5 of the quilt instructions.)

4. Follow steps 4 to 7 of the quilt instructions to assemble the appliquéd scene. See Figure 2-31 for the design layout.

5. On each facing piece, fold one lengthwise edge under $\frac{1}{4}$″ and under again $\frac{1}{4}$″. Topstitch close to edge for a clean finish.

6. Lay the facing pieces on top of the appliquéd cover, right sides together (Fig. 2-32).

7. Place the album lining, right side down, on top of the facings and cover. Pin all layers together to secure. Machine stitch around the outside edges, taking a $\frac{1}{2}$″ to $\frac{5}{8}$″ seam and leaving a 9″ opening along the lower edge to turn (Fig. 2-33). Trim the corner seam allowance to $\frac{1}{4}$″ and turn the cover right side out to check the fit. The cover should slide on easily and not be so snug as to stretch when the album is closed.

8. Remove the album and turn the cover to the wrong side. Trim away the fleece from the seam allowance and trim the stabilizer from the back to make quilting easier.

Fig. 2-28 **Photo Album**

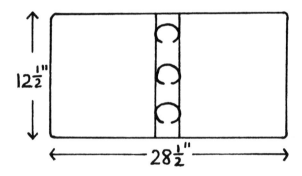

Fig. 2-29
For album cover and lining.

Fig. 2-30
For facing.

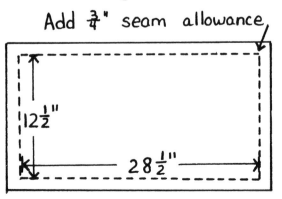

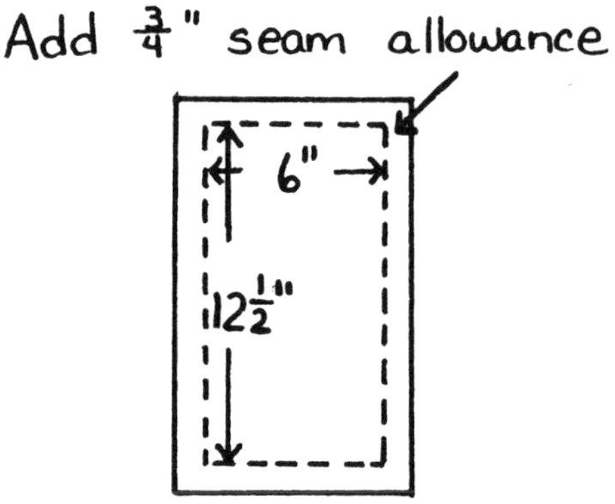

Fig. 2-31

41
*Hansel and
Gretel*

Fig. 2-32

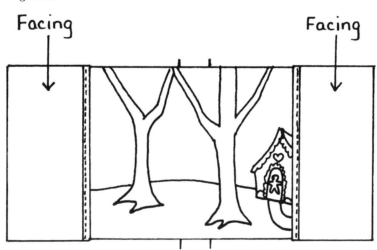

Fig. 2-33

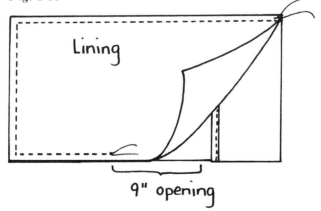

9. Turn the cover right side out and press. Slipstitch the opening closed.

10. Follow steps 23 and 24 of the quilt instructions for marking and quilting leaves. Hand quilt only around the traced leaf motifs. Additional quilting is unnecessary. *Note:* Be sure when quilting the leaves to avoid catching the facings with your stitches or you will be unable to slide the cover on your album.

11. Slip the finished cover over the album.

PATTERNS▶

Quilt
Girl's Vest
Rocking Chair Cushions
Album Cover

Path - Girl's Vest

Quilt

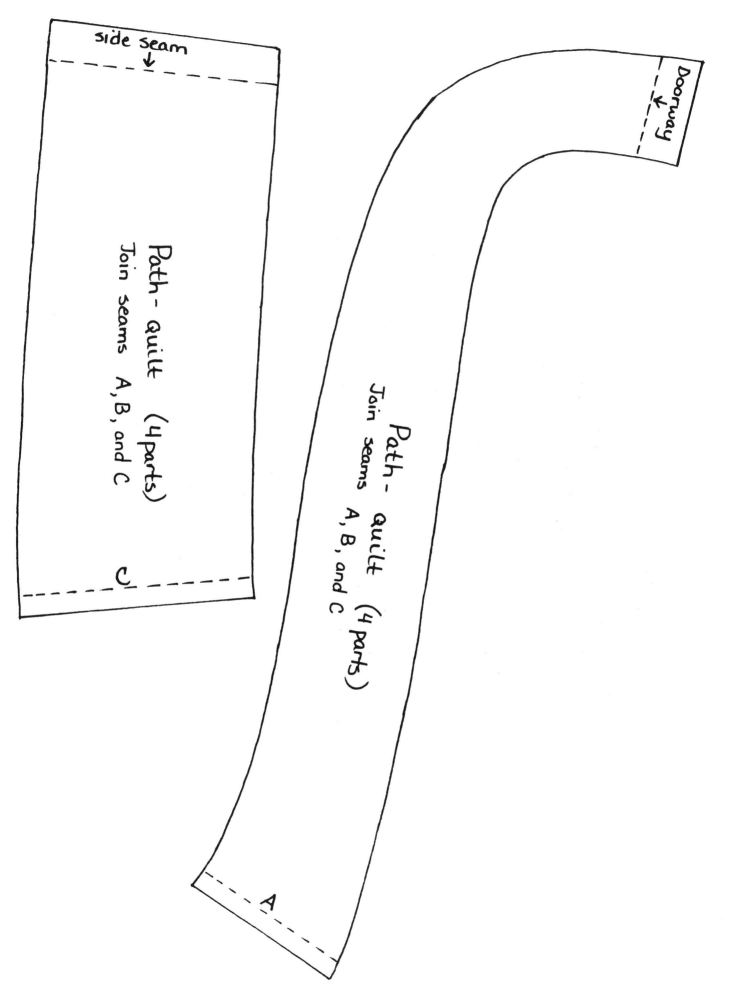

side seam

Path - quilt (4 parts)
Join seams A, B, and C

C

Doorway

Path - quilt (4 parts)
Join seams A, B, and C

A

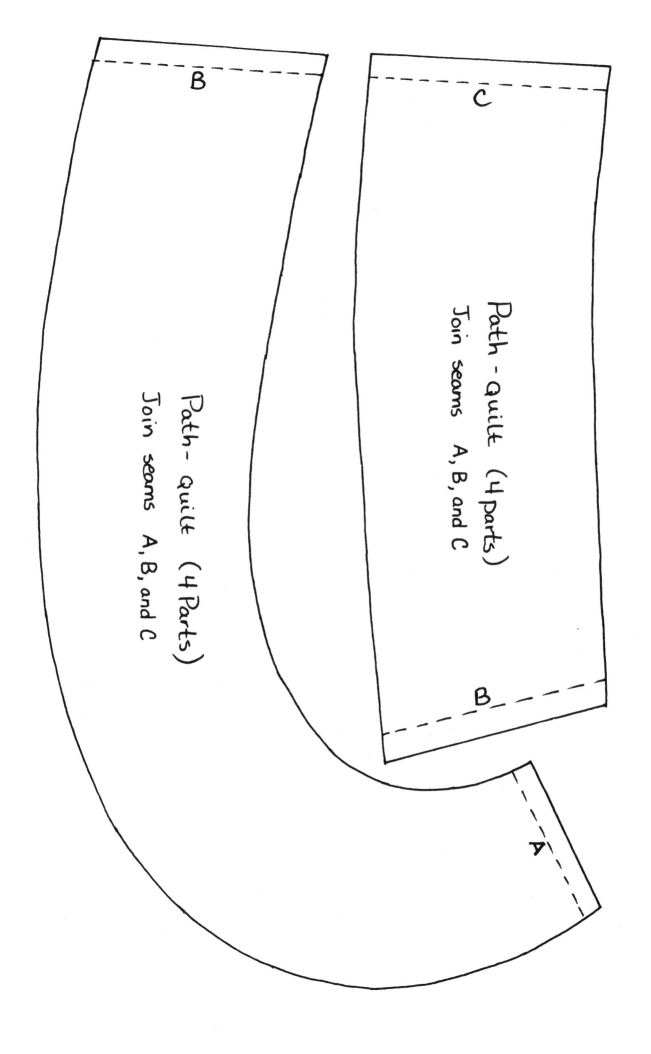

B

Path - Quilt (4 parts)
Join seams A, B, and C

C

Path - Quilt (4 Parts)
Join seams A, B, and C

B

A

46

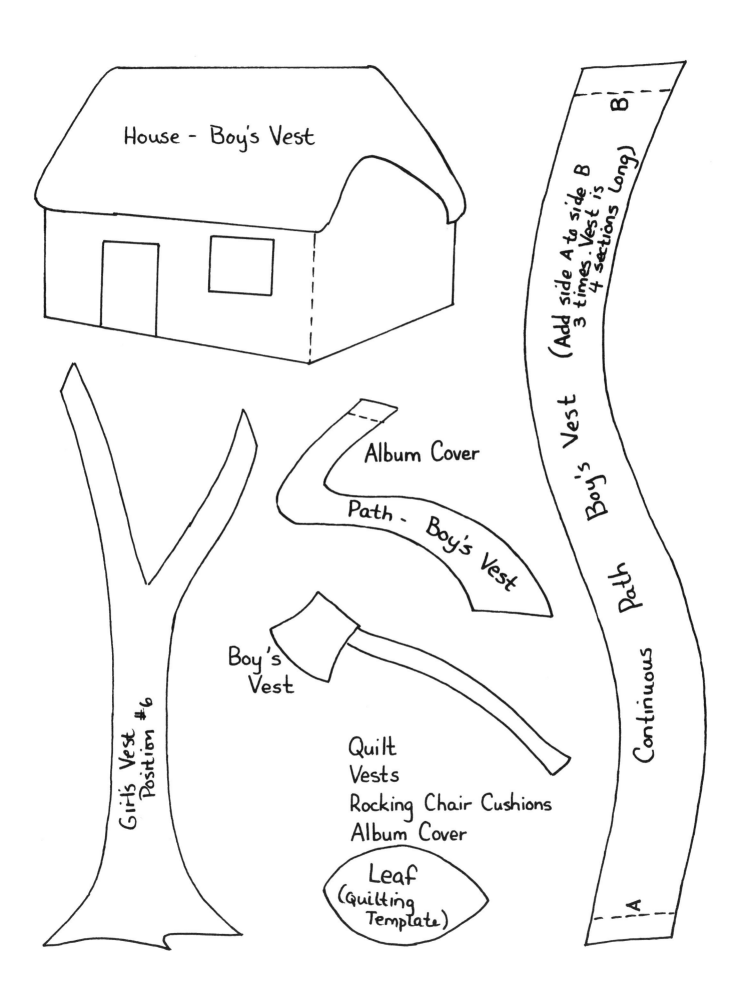

House - Boy's Vest

Album Cover

Path - Boy's Vest

Boy's Vest

Quilt
Vests
Rocking Chair Cushions
Album Cover

Leaf
(Quilting
Template)

Girl's Vest
Position #6

Boy's Vest   (Add side A to side B
3 times. Vest is
4 sections long)

B

Continuous   Path

A

47

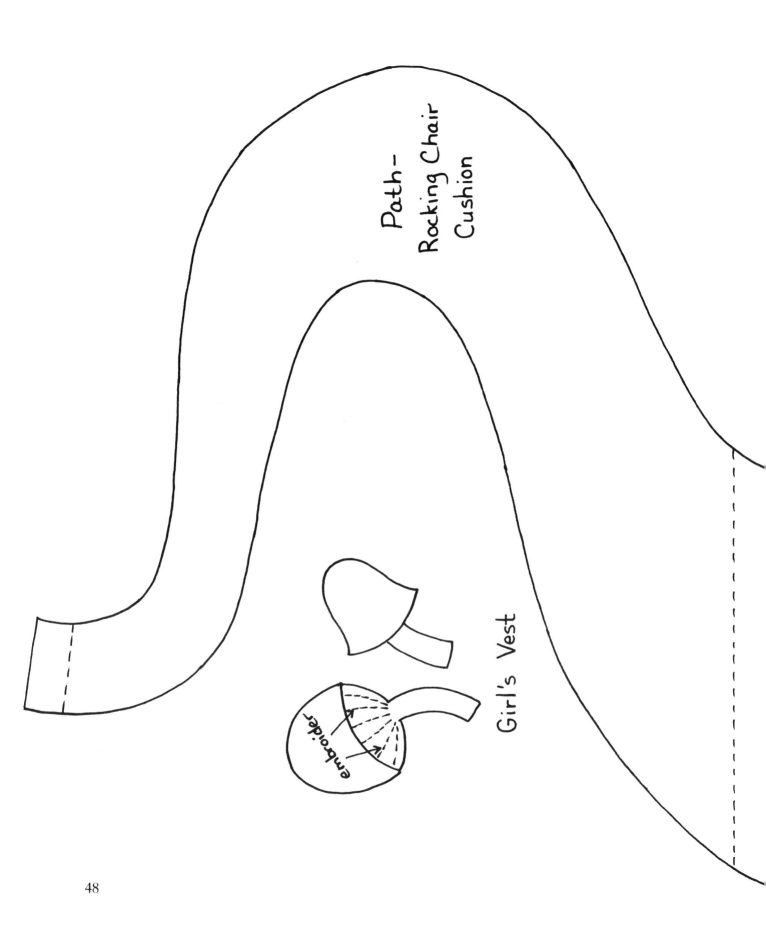

Path—
Rocking Chair
Cushion

embroider

Girl's Vest

48

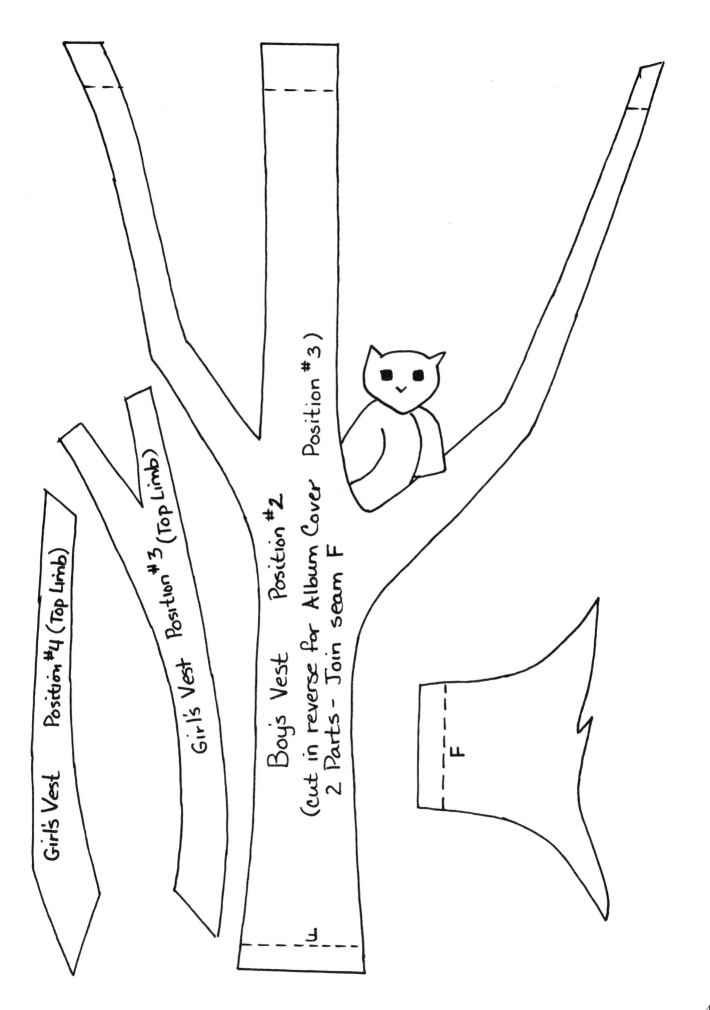

Girl's Vest Position #4 (Top Limb)

Girl's Vest Position #3 (Top Limb)

Boy's Vest Position #2
(cut in reverse for Album Cover Position #3)
2 Parts - Join seam F

F

49

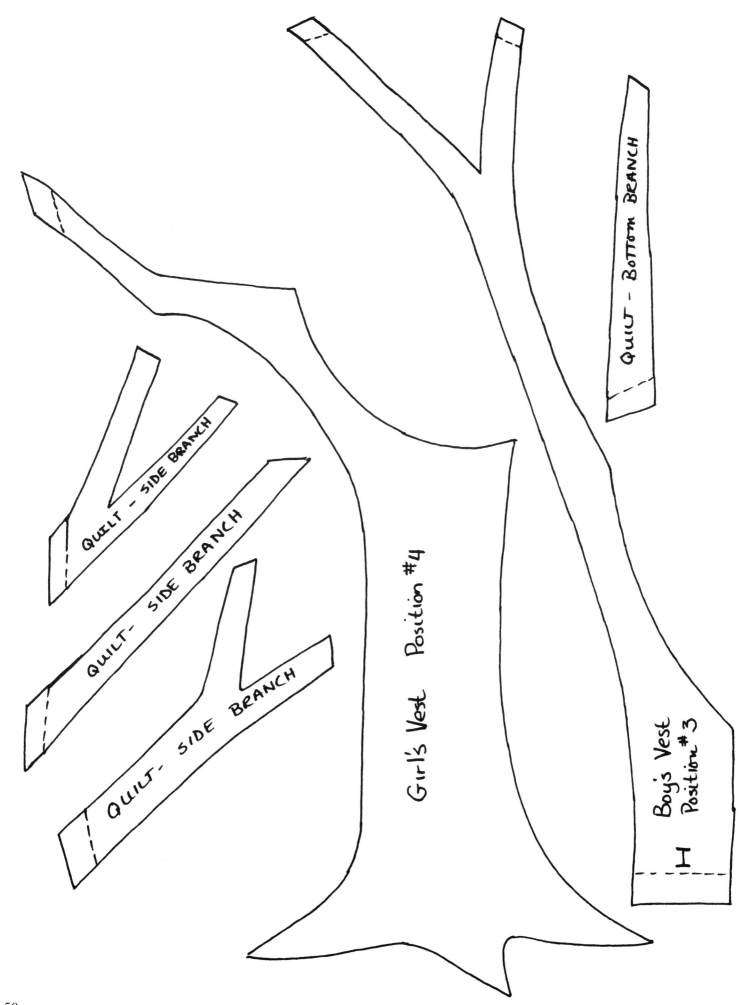

QUILT - BOTTOM BRANCH

QUILT - SIDE BRANCH

QUILT - SIDE BRANCH

QUILT - SIDE BRANCH

Girl's Vest Position #4

Boy's Vest Position #3

50

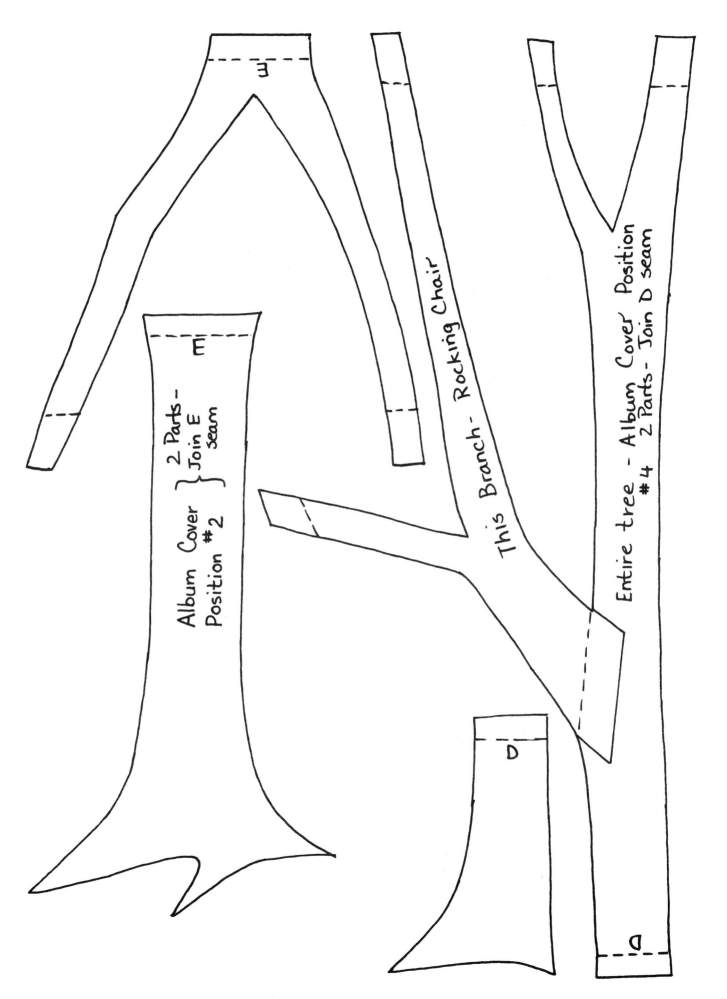

E

Album Cover – Position #2 } 2 Parts – Join E seam

E

This Branch – Rocking Chair

Entire tree – Album Cover Position #4 2 Parts– Join D seam

D

D

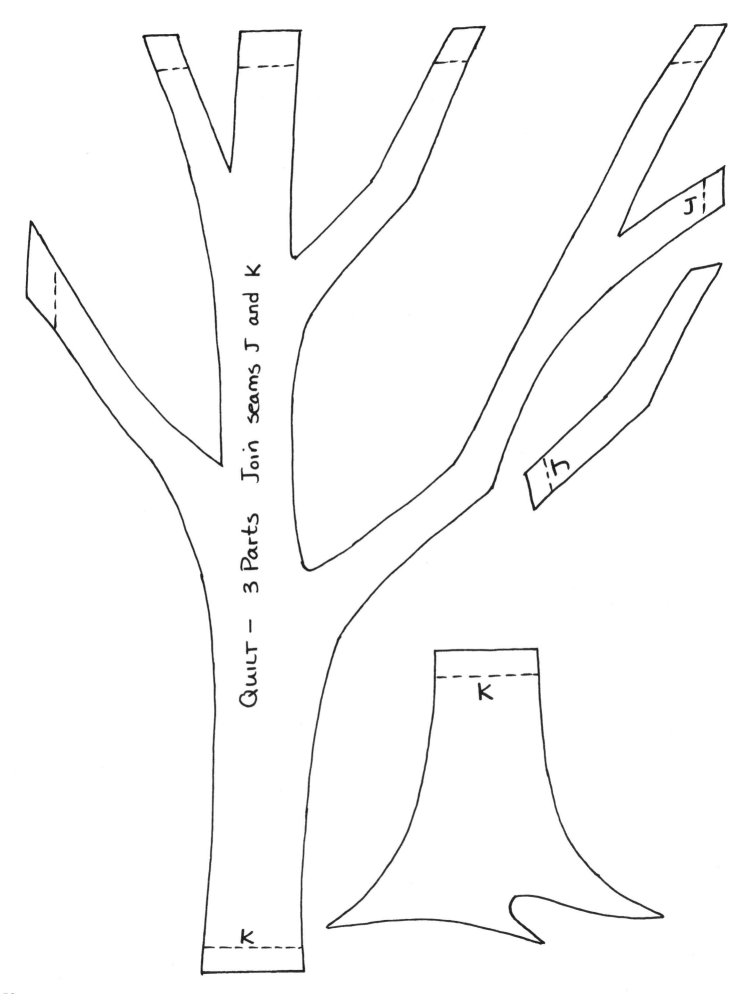

Quilt – 3 Parts   Join seams J and K

J

J

K

K

*Red Riding Hood jacket
and Wolf-Woodsman vest (front).*

*Red Riding Hood jacket
and Wolf-Woodsman vest (back).*

Red Riding Hood doll quilt and tote.

Three Little Pigs overalls and jumper.

Three Little Pigs place mats.

Three Little Pigs exercise mat.

Gingerbread Man aprons.

Rapunzel pinafore, Sleeping Beauty dress and vest, and Cinderella bib-collar.

Fairy princess pillows: Rapunzel, Sleeping Beauty, and Cinderella.

"Once Upon a Time"
Quilt.

Hansel and Gretel vests (front).   *Hansel and Gretel vests (back).*

Hansel and Gretel rocking-chair cushions and album cover.

Hansel and Gretel crib quilt.

Jack and the Beanstalk vest (back).

Jack and the Beanstalk growth chart,
drawstring bag, and trinket bag.

"Fe, Fi, Fo, Fum" quilt.

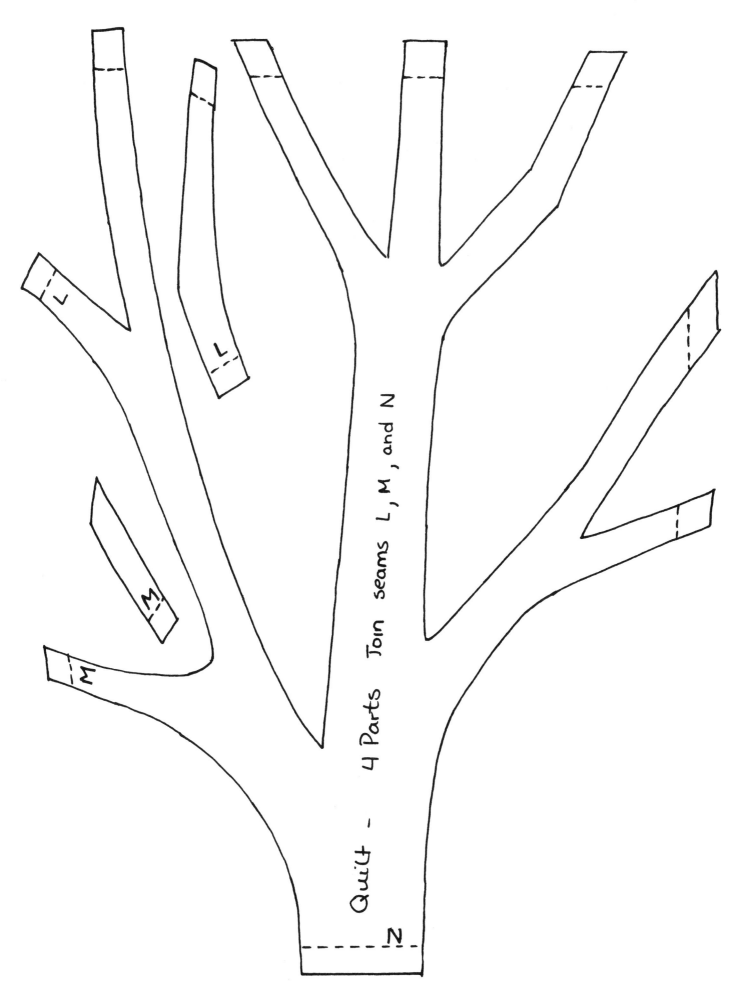

Quilt – 4 Parts Join seams L , M , and N

53

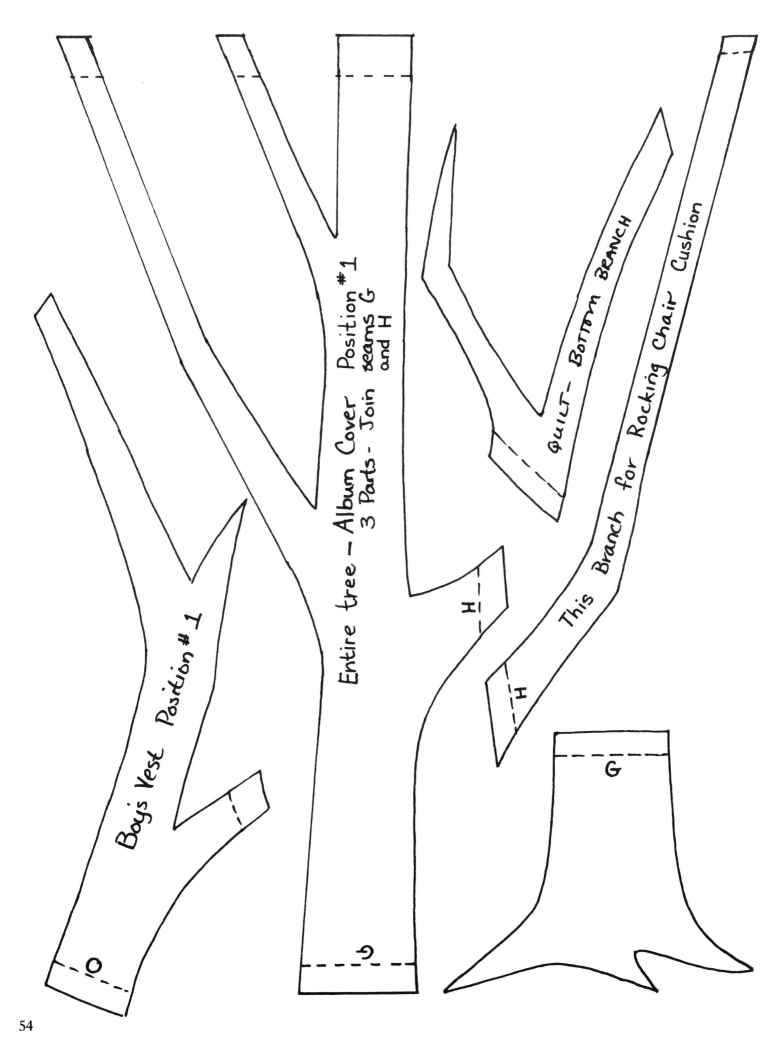

Boys Vest Position #1

O

Entire tree – Album Cover Position #1
3 Parts – Join seams G and H

G

H

H

G

Quilt – Bottom Branch

This Branch for Rocking Chair Cushion

54

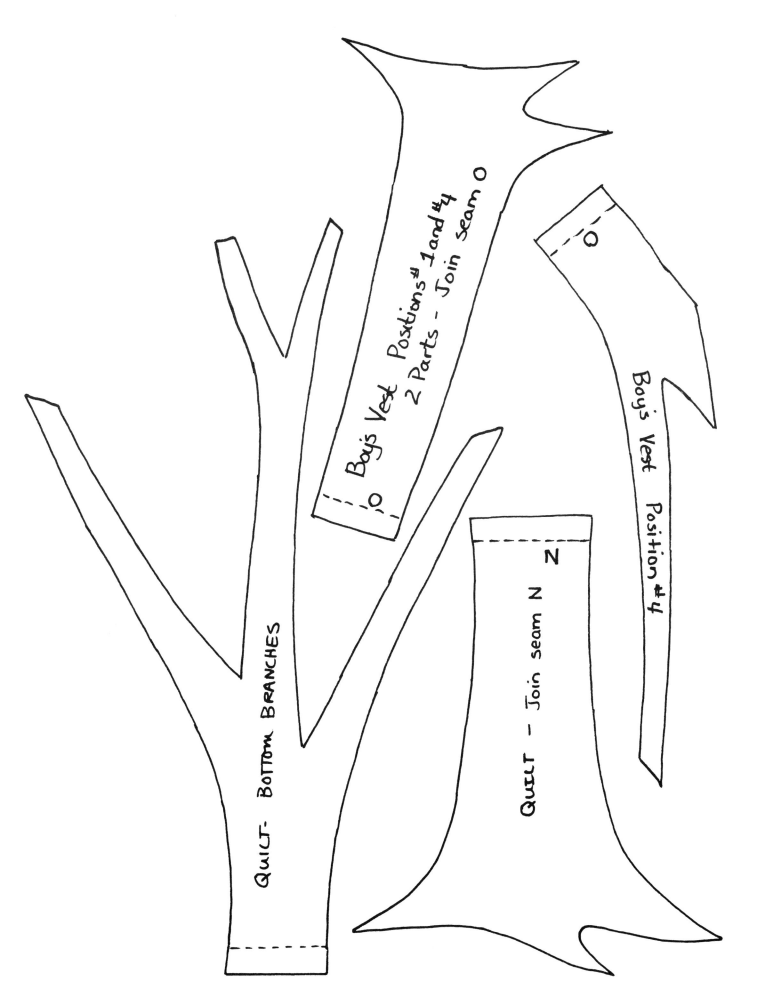

Boys Vest Postions #1 and #4
2 Parts - Join seam O

O

Boys Vest Position #4

QUILT- BOTTOM BRANCHES

QUILT - Join seam N

N

55

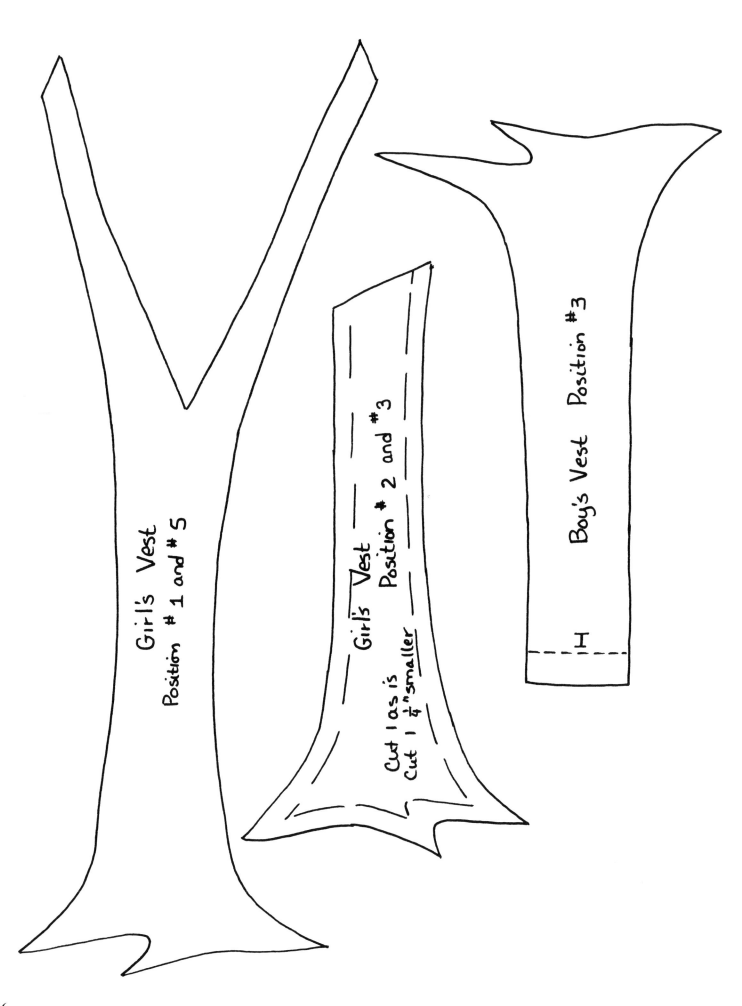

Girl's Vest
Position # 1 and # 5

Girl's Vest
Position # 2 and # 3
Cut 1 as is
Cut 1 ¼" smaller

Boy's Vest   Position #3

Chapter 3

The Gingerbread Man

Fig. 3-1
Crib quilt.

Fig. 3-2
Monogrammed aprons.

Fig. 3-3
Bib with sleeves.

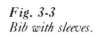

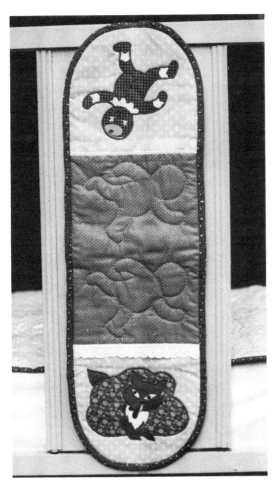

Fig. 3-4
Mother's shoulder towel.

Fig. 3-5
Diaper hanger.

Fig. 3-6
Crib toy.

Fig. 3-7
Mobile.

Capture the laughter and merriment of this favorite children's story in a colorful crib quilt and coordinating nursery accessories. Designed for either sex, this timeless ensemble is sure to be enjoyed by every member of the family.

Appliqué work can be done by hand or machine. However, we recommend using machine appliqué for these projects simply for the sake of expediency—especially if you plan on making the entire nursery ensemble. Machine appliqué is also more durable and can withstand many washings.

Crib Quilt

The finished quilt (see cover for color photograph) measures 43″ × 53″.

REQUIREMENTS

Yardage (44″ fabric):

Yellow print—2¾ yds. (31″ × 41″ center background and 45″ × 55″ lining)

Blue pindot—1 yd. (border strips)

Lightweight fusible interfacing—1 yd.

Lightweight nonfusible interfacing—1 yd. (stabilizer)

High-loft quilt batting—45″ × 55″

Assorted scraps for appliqués

Red jumbo rickrack—3 yds.

White gathered eyelet (¾″ wide)—4½ yds.

Self-made bias—⅓ yd. to make 5½ yds. of 1¼″ continuous bias

Red, white, and black embroidery floss

White embroidery floss or perle cotton for tying quilt center

White quilting thread

Matching colored thread for machine appliqué

DIRECTIONS

1. Trace the outlines of the five composite template figures onto white paper and cut out the shapes. Position these paper figures on the 31″ × 41″ background, referring to the drawing in Figure 3-8. Lightly trace around the shapes onto the background using a pencil or water-soluble marker (Fig. 3-9).

2. Lay the rickrack on top of the background fabric, forming smooth curves and connecting all the shapes. Lightly trace the path of the rickrack onto the background as you did with the appliqués in step 1 (Fig. 3-9).

3. Remove the paper templates and sew the rickrack in place. We recommend using an even-feed attachment, if your machine has one, when you apply the rickrack. It will keep the fabric from puckering as you sew around the curves. If you do not have this attachment, hand baste the rickrack in place before machine stitching. When sewing, be careful not to stretch the rickrack as you turn each curve, but ease its fullness into the curve.

4. Assemble the fused appliqué figures using a glue stick. *Do not* glue them in position on the background yet.

5. Working with just the fused appliqués, machine appliqué the spots on the

cow; the eyes, mouth, and tongue on the fox; and the hair and icing on the Gingerbread Man. Use the icing trim guide for the large template to cut one piece of white fabric. Then position that piece over the template and cut smaller pieces to fit the arms and legs. When appliquéing the icing trim, satin stitch only to $\frac{1}{8}''$ from the finished edge (Fig. 3-10). Pull the thread ends to the back side of the appliqué and make a knot so that the stitching will not unravel. (The reason for stopping $\frac{1}{8}''$ from the edge is so that the final satin

Fig. 3-8

stitching, which is done in step 7 with rust-colored thread, will be smooth and even and will not have to overlap any previous satin stitching.)

6. Mark and embroider details on the Gingerbread Man, cow, and fox and the facial details on the little old woman. Refer to the templates for the placement on each. Most details are made by satin stitching with two strands of embroidery floss. The eyes on the Gingerbread Man are made with six strands of floss. To embroider the eyes, first make a diagonal cross with $\frac{1}{2}$"-long stitches. Then make a third vertical stitch over the cross (Fig. 3-11).

7. Glue the appliqués in place on the yellow background over the traced outlines. Place a piece of nonfusible interfacing under the background area to be appliquéd. Machine appliqué with matching thread. Trim the stabilizer from the back when appliquéing is completed.

8. For the border strips, cut two pieces of blue pindot $7\frac{1}{2}$" × 41" for vertical borders and two pieces $7\frac{1}{2}$" × 44" for horizontal borders. Sew on the vertical border strips, then the horizontal border strips, taking $\frac{1}{2}$" seam allowances. Press seams toward border.

9. Straight stitch the eyelet trim along rectangular border seams using an even-

Fig. 3-9

Paper outlines pinned to background

Rickrack path traced onto background

feed attachment. If you do not have this attachment, hand baste the eyelet in place before stitching.

10. Using a pencil or water-soluble marker, mark the yellow center of the quilt top for tying, dividing it into 3″ squares (see Fig. 3-8).

11. To mark the border for quilting, use the small Gingerbread Man template and grain line 1. Mark the midpoint of each border and place the grain line of the template over each midpoint. Working from the center of each side toward the corners, evenly space the Gingerbread Man template (Fig. 3-12).

Fig. 3-10

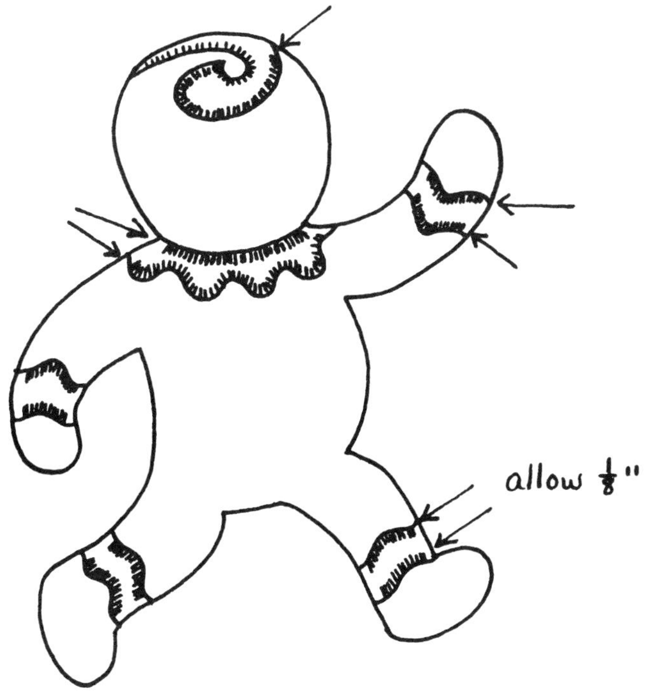

allow ⅛″

Fig. 3-11

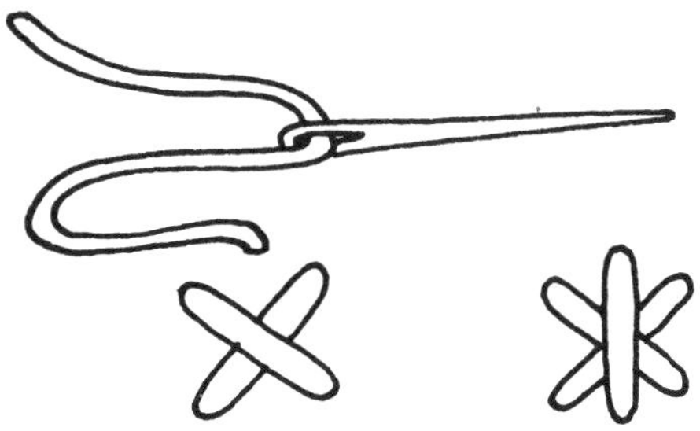

Fig. 3-12

Midpoint of border

Men evenly spaced (corner man turned to "round" corner)

Fig. 3-13

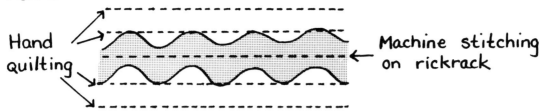

Hand quilting

Machine stitching on rickrack

12. On a flat surface, lay the lining out right side down. Spread the batting over the lining. Place the marked quilt top over the batting, smoothing out all layers. Baste the layers together $\frac{1}{2}''$ inside the eyelet trim and again along the outside edges of the border.

13. Using six strands of white embroidery floss or white perle cotton, tie the center of the quilt (see the instructions in Chapter 1 on tying).

14. Hand quilt around all the appliqué figures and along the eyelet edge of the quilt. Quilt along the outside edges of the rickrack, catching its outermost points. This will prevent the rickrack from curling when the quilt is laundered. Quilt again $\frac{1}{4}''$ from the rickrack edges (Fig. 3-13).

15. Quilt the Gingerbread Man outlines around the border.

16. Trim batting and lining edges even with quilt top and sew the continuous-bias binding (red print) around outside edges. (See the instructions in Chapter 1 on making a continuous bias, sewing to the quilt, and mitering the corners.)

Monogrammed Aprons

No matter what you are baking, your little helpers will enjoy wearing one of these aprons (see color section for photograph). Personalize the apron with the child's name for an extra-special touch. The finished aprons are approximately 19" long and 20" wide.

REQUIREMENTS

Yardage (44" fabric):

    Ecru muslin, canvas, or poplin—1 yd. (Cut lengthwise, this will make two aprons and ties.)

    Red print—$\frac{1}{8}$ yd. ($2\frac{1}{2}'' \times 15''$ strip for ruffle on girl's apron)

    Assorted fabric scraps for appliqués

    Lightweight nonfusible interfacing—$\frac{1}{2}$ yd. for two aprons (You will need this only if you are appliquéing to a lightweight fabric such as muslin.)

    Lightweight fusible interfacing—$\frac{1}{2}$ yd. for two aprons

Red-print bias binding—1 yd. per apron (Bias on girl's apron should coordinate with ruffle.)

Red medium-size rickrack—1 yd. per apron

1 pair D rings (2 cm width) for boy's apron

Coordinated thread for appliqué and sewing

DIRECTIONS

1. To make the pattern for the apron, mark a rectangle 20″ × 21″ on a large piece of paper. Make marks 6½″ in and 6½″ down from the top corners (Fig. 3-14). Connect these marks with a soft curve to form the armholes. The bottom edge of the girl's apron can also be rounded off by forming a curve beginning 3″ above the bottom corners and continuing 3″ out from them.

2. Cut out aprons from your paper pattern. For the boy's apron, cut three ties 1¾″ × 18″ and one tie 1¾″ × 3″. For the girl's apron, cut four ties 1¾″ × 18″. For both aprons, cut a name piece 3″ × 8″ (Fig. 3-15). (This piece is cut larger than necessary to allow for centering the name. Trim off the excess after appliquéing the name on the name plate.)

3. Trace the outlines of the four composite templates used on each apron onto white paper and cut out the shapes. Referring to Figure 3-16, position the paper figures on the apron background and lightly trace around each shape

Fig. 3-14

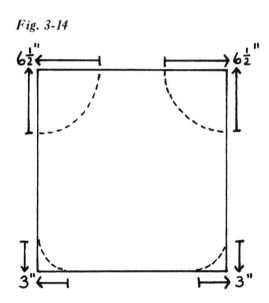

Fig. 3-15

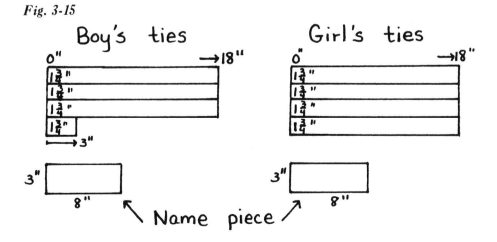

with a pencil or water-soluble marker. (For the girl's apron, substitute the little old woman for the farmer.)

4. Lay the rickrack on top of the apron, forming smooth curves and connecting all the shapes. Lightly trace the path of the rickrack onto the apron background as you did with the appliqué figures in step 3.

5. Sew the rickrack in place using the marked line as a guide. Be careful not to stretch the rickrack as you turn each curve. Ease its fullness into the curve or it will not lie flat.

6. Assemble the fused appliqué figures using a glue stick, but *do not* position them on the background fabric yet. Continue with steps 5 to 7 of the quilt instructions, omitting the directions for the fox appliqué. Use the icing trim guide for the small template. The aprons contain two appliqués not found on the quilt—the pig and the farmer. The pocket, overall straps, and hat band on the farmer and the handle of the hoe are made with a machine satin stitch. (The top of the hoe should be cut from the pattern piece.) The pig's ears are made with a machine satin stitch, and the eyes are hand embroidered. Dashed lines on the cow pattern are machine satin stitched.

7. To monogram the name on the name piece, begin by printing the letters onto the fabric with a pencil or water-soluble marker. The monogrammed name must fit into an area no larger than $2'' \times 6''$. If you think you will have difficulty in straightening and centering the letters, write the name on a piece of paper first, exactly as you want it to appear on the apron. Next, lay the fabric name piece over the paper pattern and trace the letters onto the fabric. If you cannot see the name through the fabric, darken the letters with a medium-width felt-tip marker, or tape the paper pattern to a sunlit window and hold the fabric over it to trace. Our letters measure $1'' \times \frac{3''}{4}$.

Monogram by satin stitching directly onto the fabric, following the marked letters. To prevent the fabric from puckering, pin the nonfusible interfacing under the fabric being monogrammed. It can be trimmed away once stitching

Fig. 3-16

is completed. If you are using a lightweight muslin, you will need to fuse the monogram area to fusible interfacing before monogramming.

8. Girl's apron: Cut out the ruffle strip and fold it in half lengthwise. Stitch the ends together with a $\frac{1}{2}''$ seam allowance. Clip the corners, turn, and press (Fig. 3-17A). Sew the raw edges of the strip together using two rows of machine basting $\frac{1}{4}''$ and $\frac{1}{2}''$ from the raw edges (Fig. 3-17B). Gather the strip, making a ruffle to fit the apron top. With raw edges together, pin the ruffle to the wrong side of the apron and machine baste in place (Fig. 3-18).

9. Attaching the name piece:

   Girl's apron—Pin the right side of the top edge of the name piece to the wrong side of the top edge of the apron. Keeping the raw edges even, stitch through all thicknesses, taking a $\frac{1}{2}''$ seam (Fig. 3-19). Trim seams and flip the name piece toward the front so that the ruffle stands up and the name appears on the apron front. Press the bottom edge of the name piece under $\frac{1}{2}''$ and edgestitch to the apron front (Fig. 3-20).

   Boy's apron—The name piece for the boy's apron is attached in the same manner as for the girl's apron except that there will not be a ruffle to stand up when the name piece is folded to the apron front.

10. Press the apron front under $\frac{1}{4}''$ twice along sides and lower edges, then topstitch to make a clean, finished $\frac{1}{4}''$ hem.

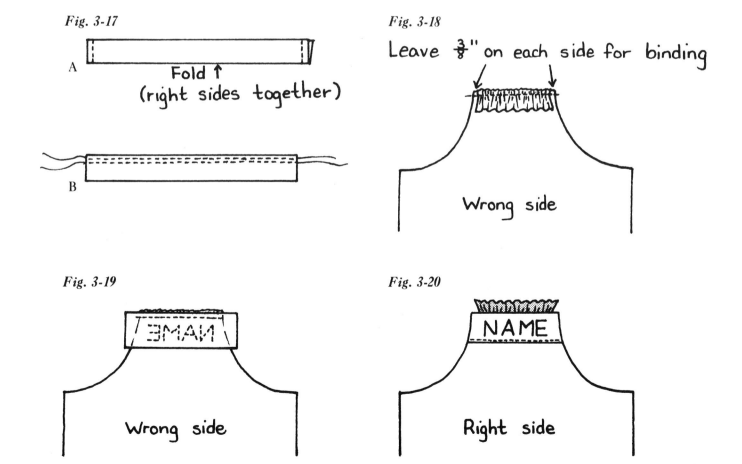

Fig. 3-17

A

Fold ↑
(right sides together)

B

Fig. 3-18

Leave $\frac{3}{8}''$ on each side for binding

Wrong side

Fig. 3-19

Wrong side

Fig. 3-20

NAME

Right side

11. Binding:

   Girl's apron—Right sides together, sew the red-print bias binding onto the armhole, leaving $\frac{1}{4}''$ seam allowances. Fold the binding back on itself at the top and bottom of the armhole so that the raw edges will not show (Fig. 3-21). When stitching is complete, fold the binding over to the back, turning the raw edge under $\frac{1}{4}''$. Edgestitch binding from the front through all thicknesses, catching folded edge on the reverse side.

   Boy's apron—Right sides together, sew the binding to the top edge of the apron leaving $\frac{1}{4}''$ seam allowances. Fold the binding to the back of the apron, turning under $\frac{1}{4}''$. Edgestitch the binding from the front through all thicknesses (Fig. 3-22). Bind armholes as described for girl's apron.

12. Straps: Fold the short ends of the strips in $\frac{1}{4}''$ (Fig. 3-23A). Fold the strips in half lengthwise and press. Open the strips and press the raw edges in toward the center fold (Fig. 3-23B). Fold again and edgestitch through all thicknesses for a clean finish (Fig. 3-23C).

   Sew the straps to the wrong side of the apron sides and top edges and reinforce with a stitched X (Fig. 3-24). For the boy's apron, sew the 3″ loop to the right side of the apron and attach the D rings before stitching down (Fig. 3-25). The loops should extend $\frac{1}{2}''$ from the binding. Sew the long strap to the left side of the apron top. Pull the long strap through the D rings to finish (Fig. 3-26).

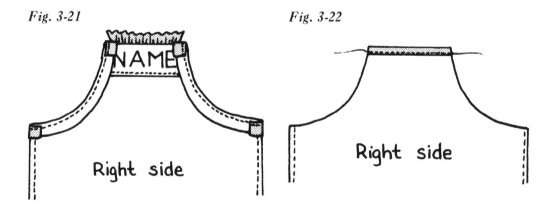

Fig. 3-21

Fig. 3-22

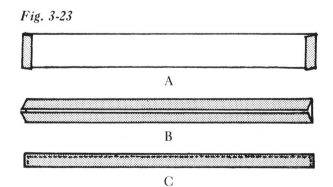

Fig. 3-23

A

B

C

Fig. 3-24

69
*The Gingerbread
Man*

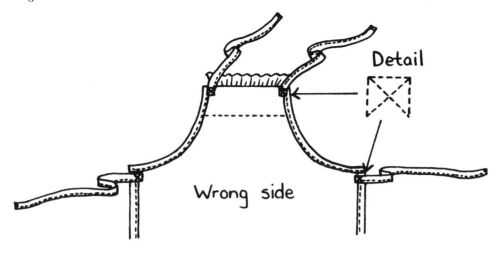

Detail

Wrong side

Fig. 3-25

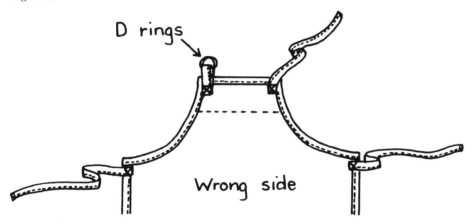

D rings

Wrong side

Fig. 3-26

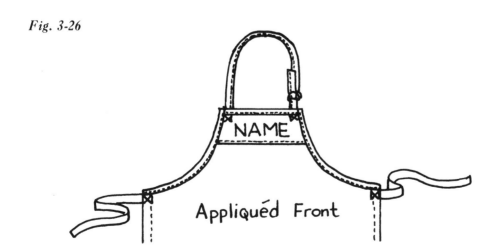

NAME

Appliquéd Front

Bib with Sleeves

Protect your baby's front and sleeves with a bib (see cover for color photograph). This attractive coverup will fit a child six to twelve months of age.

REQUIREMENTS

Yardage (44″ fabric):

Yellow print—$\frac{1}{2}$ yd. (13″ square)

Blue pindot—$\frac{1}{2}$ yd.

White flannel for lining—$\frac{1}{2}$ yd. (13″ square)

Lightweight nonfusible interfacing—$\frac{1}{2}$ yd. (13″ square)

Fleece or needlepunch batting—13″ square

Lightweight fusible interfacing—6″ square

Assorted fabric scraps for appliqués

Red medium-size rickrack—18″

White gathered eyelet—$\frac{1}{2}$ yd.

$\frac{1}{4}$″ elastic—$\frac{1}{4}$ yd.

Red-print bias binding—$2\frac{1}{4}$ yds.

Red, black, and white embroidery floss

Coordinated thread for sewing and machine appliqué

White embroidery floss or perle cotton for tying

Fig. 3-27
Bib front and sleeve. Measurements include $\frac{1}{4}$″ seam allowance.

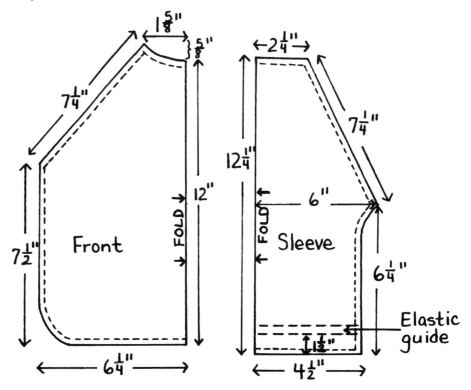

1. Draft a paper pattern for the bib, using the measurements in Figure 3-27.
2. From the yellow print, white flannel, nonfusible interfacing, and fleece or needlepunch batting, cut the bib front. From the blue pindot, cut two sleeves. Cut out the small Gingerbread Man template, using grain line #2.
3. Using the photo of the bib as a guide, position the small Gingerbread Man template and rickrack on the bib front (see steps 1 to 6 of the quilt instructions, but use the icing trim guide for the small template).
4. Sandwich the fleece layer between the yellow top and the nonfusible interfacing. Hand baste layers together around the outside edges to prevent shifting. Machine appliqué the Gingerbread Man in place on the bib front through all layers. Trim away the stabilizer from the back.
5. Baste the flannel lining to the wrong side of the bib.
6. With right sides together, stitch the front half of the raglan sleeve to the bib (Fig. 3-28).
7. Hem the sleeve edge at the wrist by turning it under $\frac{1}{4}''$ twice and topstitching close to the edge.
8. From the blue pindot, cut two strips of fabric $1'' \times 4\frac{1}{2}''$ to form a casing for the elastic. Press the short ends under $\frac{1}{4}''$, then press the long ends under $\frac{1}{4}''$ (Fig. 3-29). Edgestitch the casing in place $1''$ from the hemmed edge of the sleeve. Draw $3''$ of elastic through the casing and secure the ends with machine stitching (Fig. 3-30).
9. Sew the bias binding over the back raglan edges to finish the seams (Fig. 3-31).
10. Right sides together, stitch the underarm seams.
11. Sew the binding around the sides and lower edge of the bib front, beginning and ending $1''$ beyond the raglan seam under sleeve (Fig. 3-32).
12. Sew the binding around the neck edge leaving $12''$ of binding on each side for the ties (Fig. 3-33A). Fold the lengthwise edges of the ties to the center of the strip, then press the folded edges together to clean-finish them (Fig. 3-33B). Edgestitch close to the folded edges.

Fig. 3-28   *Fig. 3-29*

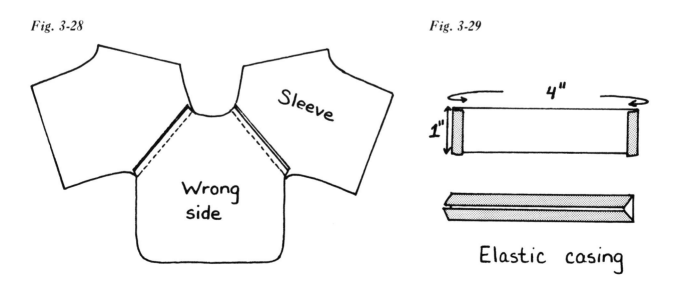

Sleeve

Wrong side

4"

1"

Elastic casing

Fig. 3-30

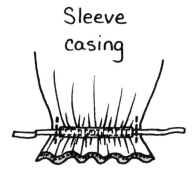

Sleeve
casing

Fig. 3-31

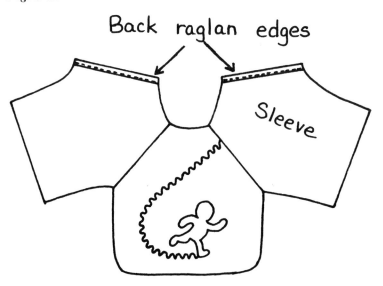

Back raglan edges

Sleeve

Fig. 3-32

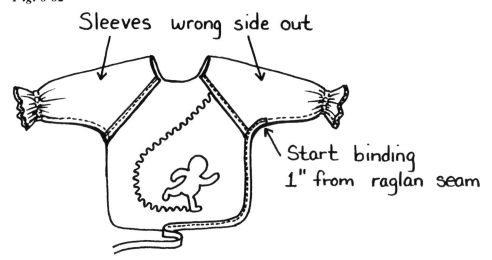

Sleeves wrong side out

Start binding
1" from raglan seam

Fig. 3-33

73
The Gingerbread Man

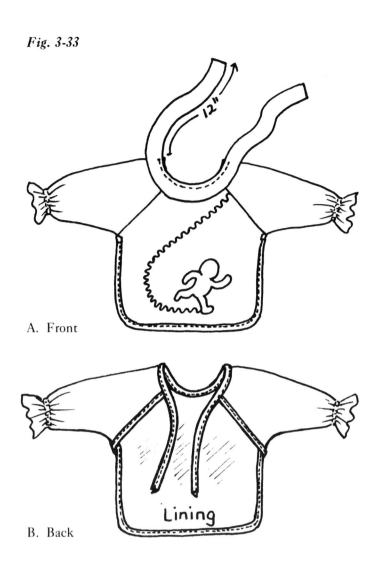

A. Front

B. Back

13. Straight stitch the gathered eyelet trim along the front raglan seams, turning ends under $\frac{1}{4}''$.
14. Mark the bib front into 3″ squares and tie with six strands of embroidery floss or perle cotton.

Mother's Shoulder Towel

Make the mother's shoulder towel (see cover for color photograph) to accompany the child's bib—a perfect duo as a shower gift. The finished size is $7\frac{1}{2}'' \times 24\frac{1}{2}''$.

REQUIREMENTS
Yardage (44″ fabric):

Yellow print—two $7\frac{1}{2}''$ squares
Blue pindot—$7\frac{1}{2}'' \times 11\frac{1}{2}''$ rectangle
Fleece—$8\frac{1}{2}'' \times 25\frac{1}{2}''$ rectangle
Lightweight fusible interfacing—$\frac{1}{4}$ yd.

Lightweight nonfusible interfacing—two $8\frac{1}{2}''$ squares
White flannel for lining—$8\frac{1}{2}'' \times 25\frac{1}{2}''$ rectangle
Assorted scraps for appliqués
Red bias binding—3 yds.
Red, white, and black embroidery floss
White quilting thread
Coordinated thread for appliqué and sewing

DIRECTIONS

1. Cut the squares and rectangles from the fabrics.
2. Fold the two $7\frac{1}{2}''$ yellow squares in half. Mark and cut a round corner. Cut both squares along the same curve so that they match (Fig. 3-34).
3. Right sides together, straight stitch the yellow sections to the short ends of the blue-pindot rectangle with a $\frac{1}{2}''$ seam allowance (Fig. 3-35).
4. Sandwich the fleece between the top and the nonfusible interfacing. Baste the layers together around the outside edges (Fig. 3-36).
5. Using grain line #2, prepare the appliqués for the small Gingerbread Man and small fox as described in the instructions in Chapter 1 for machine appliqué. Embroider all details before appliquéing. See steps 5 and 6 of quilt instructions. Be sure to use the icing trim guide for the small template.
6. Pin or glue-stick appliqués in place on the end sections and satin stitch around edges (Fig. 3-37). Trim interfacing from the wrong side.
7. Straight stitch the eyelet trim along the blue/yellow seams.
8. Baste the flannel to the wrong side along the outside edges.
9. Mark and quilt the center section of the towel. Use the small Gingerbread

Fig. 3-34

Fig. 3-35

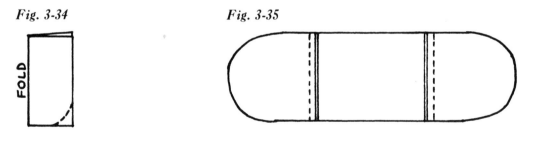

Fig. 3-36

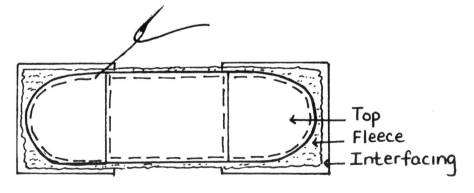

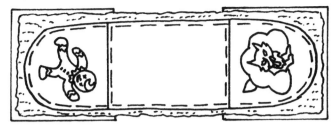

Man template turned sideways to mark the quilting design (Fig. 3-38). Trim lining and fleece to match rounded edges.

10. Sew the red bias binding around the outside edges to finish.

Diaper Hanger

There goes the Gingerbread Man again! This time he's running across the front of a diaper hanger—a very practical and colorful accessory. The finished diaper hanger (see cover for color photograph) measures 13″ × 16″.

REQUIREMENTS

Yardage (44″ fabric):

    Yellow print—1¼ yds. (22″ × 44″ rectangle for background and 9½″ × 14″ rectangle for bottom, plus two yoke pieces from template A)

    Blue pindot—½ yd. (two yoke pieces from template A)

    High-loft batting—7″ × 15″ rectangle

    Lightweight fusible interfacing—¼ yd.

    Lightweight nonfusible interfacing (stabilizer)—¼ yd.

    Assorted scraps for appliqués

Red-print bias binding—1¼ yd.

Red medium-size rickrack—1 yd.

Coordinated thread for machine appliqué and sewing

Red, white, and black embroidery floss

White quilting thread

Child-size coat hanger—12″ from end to end

Medium-weight cardboard—8½″ × 13″ rectangle

DIRECTIONS

1. Cut from yellow print one rectangle 22″ × 44″ for the background and one rectangle 9½″ × 14″ for the bottom.

2. Fold the 22″ × 44″ yellow background in half crosswise and press. Open it out and lay the fabric right side down on a flat work space. Fold the short ends in to meet the center fold (Fig. 3-39). Right sides will be facing up.

3. Using a pencil or water-soluble marker, mark two lines from the top to the bottom of the fabric 6½″ from the center on both sides (Fig. 3-40). The center area within these marked lines is the design area for all appliqués and is the front side of the diaper hanger.

75

4. Arrange the fused appliqué pieces (small templates) and rickrack on the fabric (Fig. 3-41). Using a pencil or water-soluble marker, trace around the appliqués and rickrack to mark their position.

5. Remove the appliqués and machine stitch the rickrack in place (see step 3 of the quilt instructions).

6. Embroider the details on the cow and Gingerbread Man (see step 5 of the quilt instructions, but use the icing trim guide for the small template).

7. Match the appliqués with the marked background positions. Placing stabilizer under the background area to be appliquéd, machine appliqué them in place through the front panels only. Trim stabilizer from wrong side when appliquéing is completed.

8. Finish the front edges with the red-print bias binding.

9. Along the center front of the diaper hanger, baste the left and right bound edges about $1\frac{1}{2}''$ from top and bottom. This will align the center front and prevent shifting when you attach the yoke and bottom sections (Fig. 3-42).

10. With pins, form a continuous row of $\frac{1}{4}''$ tucks along the top edge of the background. Make these tucks approximately $\frac{7}{8}''$ apart and fold them in the same direction all the way around the top. Machine stitch the tucks in place $\frac{1}{2}''$ from the top edge (Fig. 3-43).

Fig. 3-39

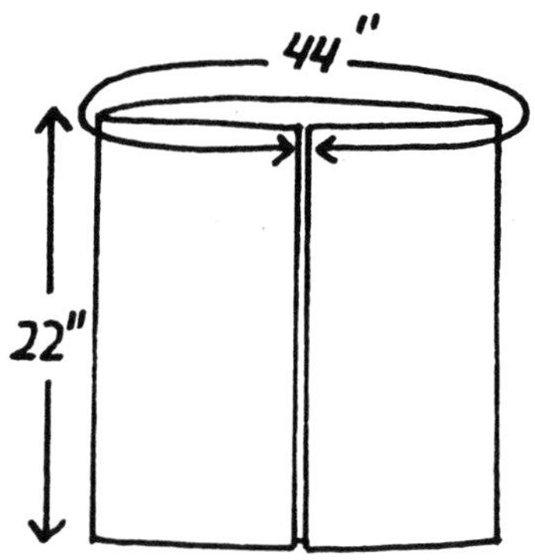

Fig. 3-40

Fig. 3-41

Fig. 3-42

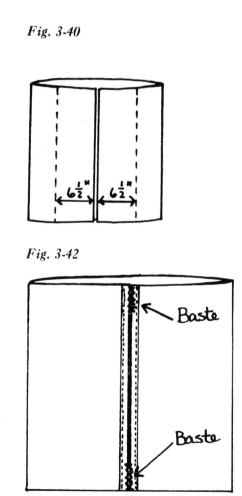

11. Preparing the yoke: Cut two pieces from the blue pindot and two pieces from the yellow print using template A. Mark one blue-pindot yoke for quilting, tracing the quilting lines from template A.

12. Baste together the marked blue yoke, the high-loft batting, and one yellow yoke. The right sides of the prints will face out. Quilt along the marked lines through all layers.

13. Machine baste $\frac{3}{8}''$ along the outside edges of the quilted yoke to keep the raw edges together.

14. Wrong sides together, pin the second set of blue and yellow yokes together. Machine baste $\frac{3}{8}''$ around the outside edges. (This double back yoke will add durability, and the yellow-print lining will match the front yoke lining.)

15. With right sides together (blue side to blue side), sew the front yoke to the back yoke along the curved top edge, taking a $\frac{1}{2}''$ seam and leaving a $1''$ opening at the center top for the coat hanger (Fig. 3-44).

16. Trim the batting away from the seam allowance close to the seam, and clip the curves. Wrong side out, mark the center front and center back of the yoke with a pencil.

17. Right sides together, ease the tucked background edge to fit the yoke, matching the markings for the center fronts and center back. Straight stitch, taking a $\frac{1}{2}''$ seam (Fig. 3-45). Turn the yoke right side out.

18. Straight stitch the eyelet trim over the bottom edge of the yoke, keeping the yoke seam pressed toward the yoke.

19. Mark and clip ($\frac{3}{8}''$) the lower edge of the yellow background from the center front $6\frac{1}{2}''$ and again $8\frac{1}{2}''$ from these first markings (Fig. 3-46). The four clips on this lower edge will correspond to the four corners of the bottom of the hanger. Match the corners with the clip marks, right sides together, and sew together, taking a $\frac{1}{2}''$ seam (Fig. 3-47).

20. Turn the hanger right side out and insert the $8\frac{1}{2}'' \times 13''$ piece of cardboard in the bottom.

Fig. 3-43

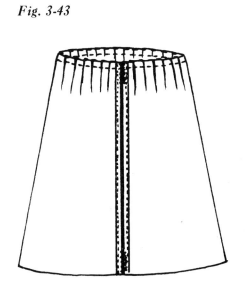

Fig. 3-44

Fig. 3-45

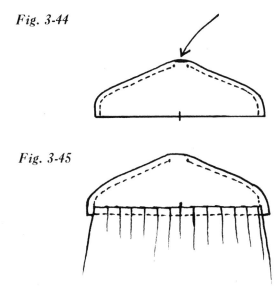

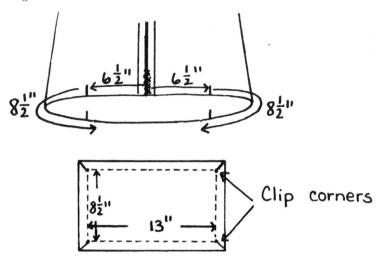

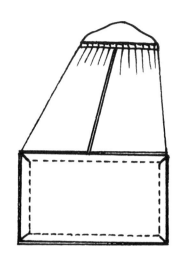

Crib Toy

You *can* catch the Gingerbread Man in this three-dimensional stuffed crib toy (see cover for color photograph). This little fellow makes a perfect last-minute gift or bazaar item. If you are really ambitious, you can make four or five gingerbread men from the smaller template and string them together with ribbon to hang over a crib or playpen (Fig. 3-48). The smaller template can also be used to make Christmas tree ornaments. The directions for making this stuffed toy for any of these uses are essentially the same. The large-size toy measures 6″ × 8″ when stuffed.

REQUIREMENTS

Yardage (44″ fabric):

    Rust print—10″ × 20″ rectangle

    Solid white—scrap

    Solid blue—scrap

    Lightweight fusible interfacing—scrap

Polyester fiberfill for stuffing

Red, white, and black embroidery floss

Matching thread for sewing and machine appliqué

DIRECTIONS

1. Cut the rust-print 10″ × 20″ rectangle and fold it in half crosswise, right sides together.
2. Trace the large Gingerbread Man template onto the fabric and add a scant $\frac{1}{2}$″ seam allowance around the outside edges.
3. Fuse the white scrap fabric and cut two icing collars and enough zigzag icing

for the front and back of the Gingerbread Man's arms and legs. Fuse the blue fabric for the hair.

4. Machine appliqué the icing and hair to the Gingerbread Man front and back (Fig. 3-49).

5. Mark and embroider the details on face and tummy as described in step 5 of the quilt instructions.

6. Right sides together, stitch front to back, taking a $\frac{1}{2}''$ seam and leaving a $2\frac{1}{2}''$ opening at the top of the head for turning.

Fig. 3-48

Fig. 3-49

Front   Back

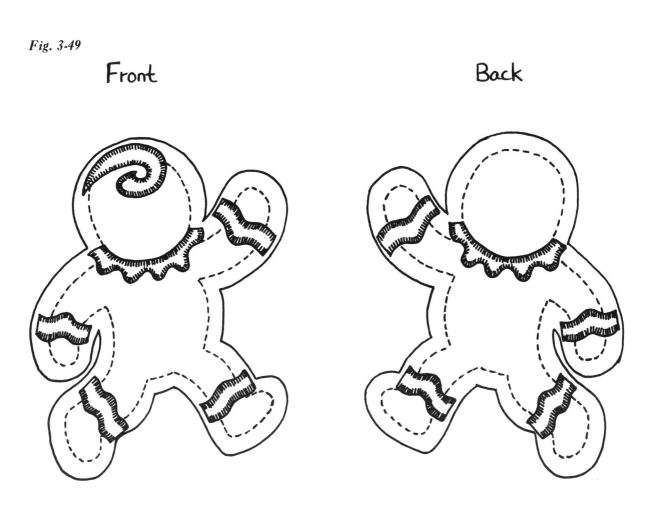

7. Trim seam allowances to $\frac{1}{4}''$ and clip all curves.
8. Turn right side out and stuff. Slipstitch the opening closed.

Mobile

Let your little one watch the Gingerbread Man in action as he swings above the crib on this cheerful mobile (see cover for color photograph).

REQUIREMENTS

12″ wooden hoop
18″ square of $\frac{1}{4}''$ oak veneer or $\frac{1}{8}''$ to $\frac{1}{4}''$ balsa wood. (The balsa wood can be found at craft supply stores. Lumberyards usually sell veneer scraps.)
One large wooden bead, as used for macramé
Wood glue or other thick-white crafts glue
Assorted colors of acrylic paint to match fabric
Yardage (44″ fabric):
    Blue Pindot—$\frac{1}{4}$ yd. ($3\frac{1}{2}''$ × 48″ rectangle to be pieced)
    Fusible interfacing—$\frac{1}{2}$ yd.
    Assorted fabric scraps (the same as used in quilt)
    Fleece scraps
$\frac{3}{8}''$ grosgrain ribbon—6 yds.
$\frac{1}{4}''$ grosgrain ribbon—$2\frac{1}{4}$ yds. (bows)
Red medium-size rickrack—$1\frac{1}{2}$ yds.
Coordinated sewing thread
Red, white and black embroidery floss

DIRECTIONS

1. Trace the outlines of the seven small template figures onto the oak veneer or balsa wood. The oak veneer will need to be cut with a band saw. (Some lumberyards can do this for you.) The balsa wood can be cut with an X-acto knife.
2. Sand the edges of the wooden shapes until they are smooth. If desired, paint the edges with colors to match the fabrics, which will be glued on the flat sides.

Fig. 3-50

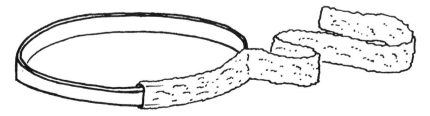

3. Cut six lengths of $\frac{3}{8}''$ grosgrain ribbon 6″ long and one length 22″ long. Glue one end to the top of each wooden figure except for the tree, which will hang from the center on the 22″ ribbon. Fused fabrics will be glued over the ribbons.

4. Fuse all fabrics to the fusible interfacing before cutting.

5. Assemble the fused fabrics as you would for machine appliqué. You will not need to satin stitch them in place, however. A light touch of glue behind each piece is all that is required. Embroider the eyes, nose, and mouth on the little old woman before gluing her face in place. All other details, which were formerly embroidered, can be duplicated by gluing small scraps of fabric in their place.

6. To prepare the hoop and to give it a soft, padded look, glue a layer of fleece around the outside and over the top and bottom edges (Fig. 3-50). Hold the fleece in place with five or six clothespins until the glue dries.

7. Machine stitch the rickrack down the center of the $3\frac{1}{2}'' \times 48''$ strip. Press under $\frac{1}{2}''$ along one length of the strip (Fig. 3-51). Wrap the strip over the hoop so that the rickrack runs along the outside of the hoop. On the inside of the hoop, pin the folded edge over the raw edge. Slipstitch the folded edge closed (Fig. 3-52). Overlap the short ends and fold the top end under $\frac{1}{2}''$. Slipstitch this short end closed for a clean finish (Fig. 3-53).

8. With a measuring tape, measure the inside perimeter of the ring and divide the distance by six. Mark these points on the hoop with straight pins or a chalk pencil.

9. Cut six 21″ lengths of $\frac{3}{8}''$ grosgrain ribbon. Hand stitch these securely over the markings on the inside of the hoop. Thread the six ribbon ends, along

Fig. 3-51

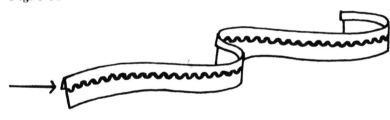

Fig. 3-52

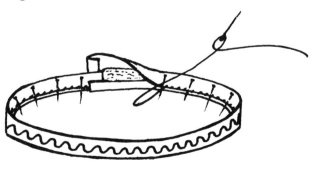

Fig. 3-53

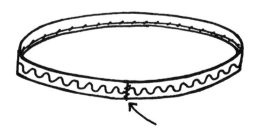

Fig. 3-54

Fig. 3-55

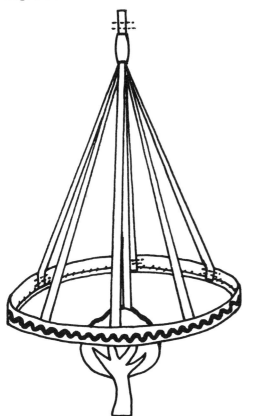

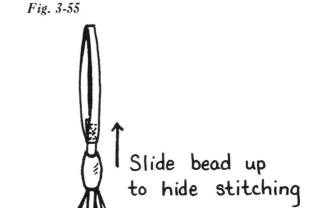

Slide bead up to hide stitching

with the 22″ ribbon with tree attached, through the large wooden bead and stitch the ribbon ends together 1″ from the top (Fig. 3-54).

10. Cut a 24″ length of ⅜″ ribbon. Fold the ribbon in half and sew the raw ends over the cluster of ribbons at the top. Slide the wooden bead in place over the stitching where the ribbons join (Fig. 3-55).

11. Stitch the 6″ lengths of ribbon, with figures attached, to the inside of the hoop over the first set of ribbons. Alternate the heights of the figures by adjusting the lengths of the ribbons from 3″ to 5″. This will add depth to the mobile and also create a feeling of movement.

12. From the ¼″ grosgrain ribbon, make seven small bows. Sew bows in place on the ribbons along the top of the hoop (see Fig. 3-7).

PATTERNS▶

Quilt

83

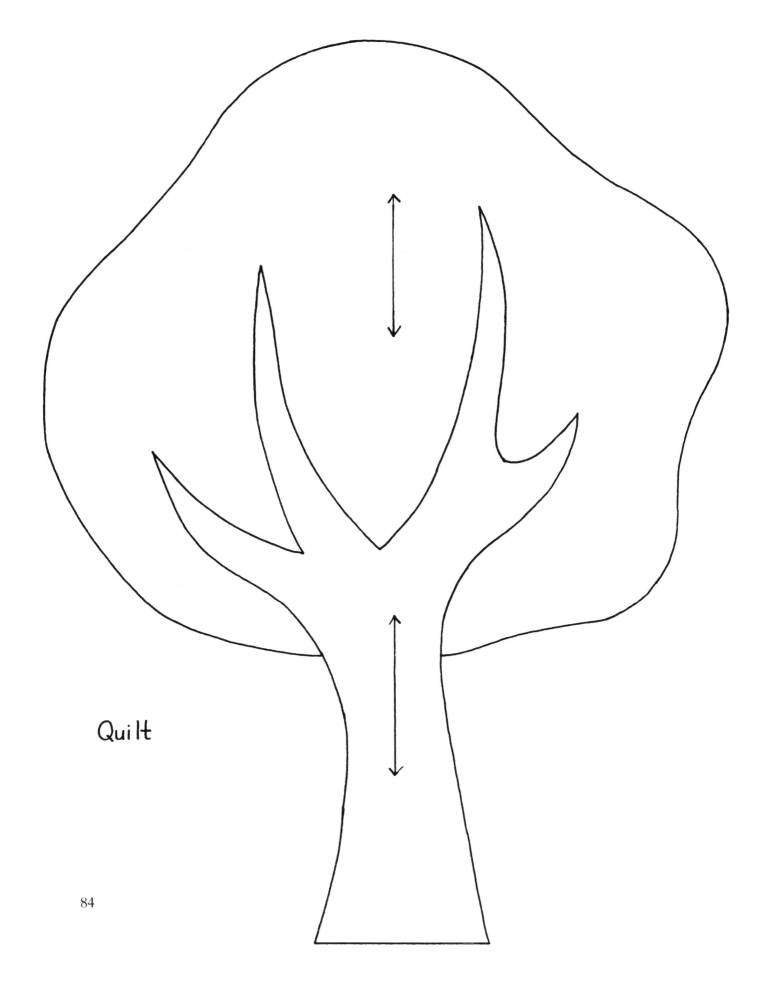

Quilt

84

Quilt

Quilt
Crib Toy

Quilt

87

Girl's Apron
Mobile

Boy's Apron
Girl's Apron
Mobile

Boy's Apron
Mobile

Boy's Apron   Diaper Hanger
Girl's Apron   Mobile

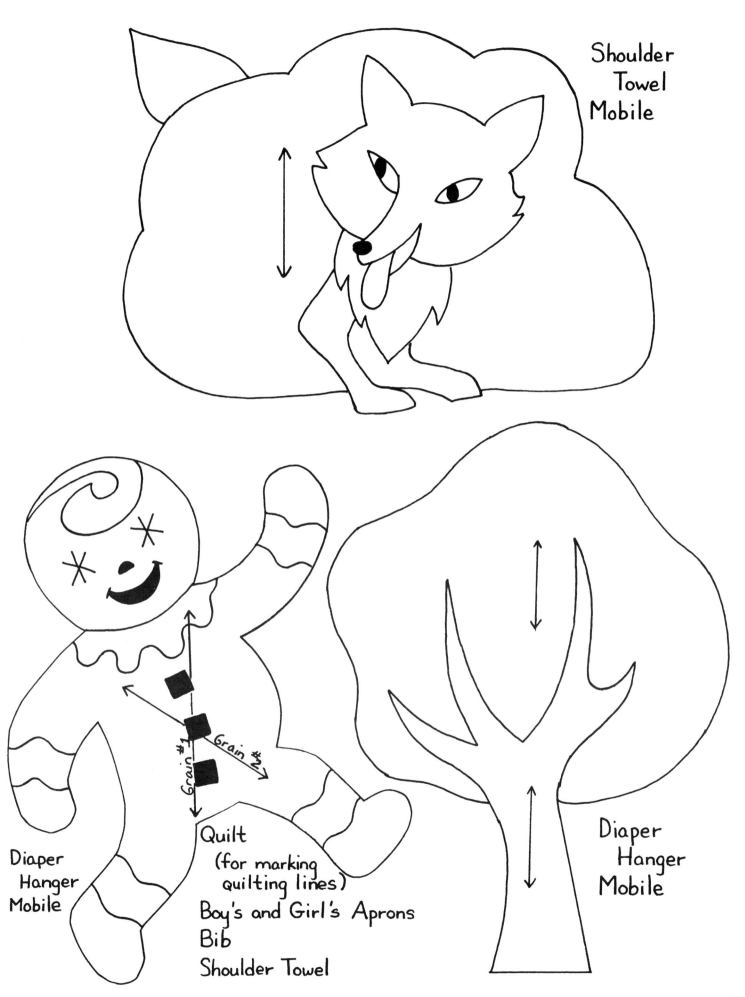

Shoulder
Towel
Mobile

Grain #1

Grain #2

Diaper
Hanger
Mobile

Quilt
(for marking
quilting lines)
Boy's and Girl's Aprons
Bib
Shoulder Towel

Diaper
Hanger
Mobile

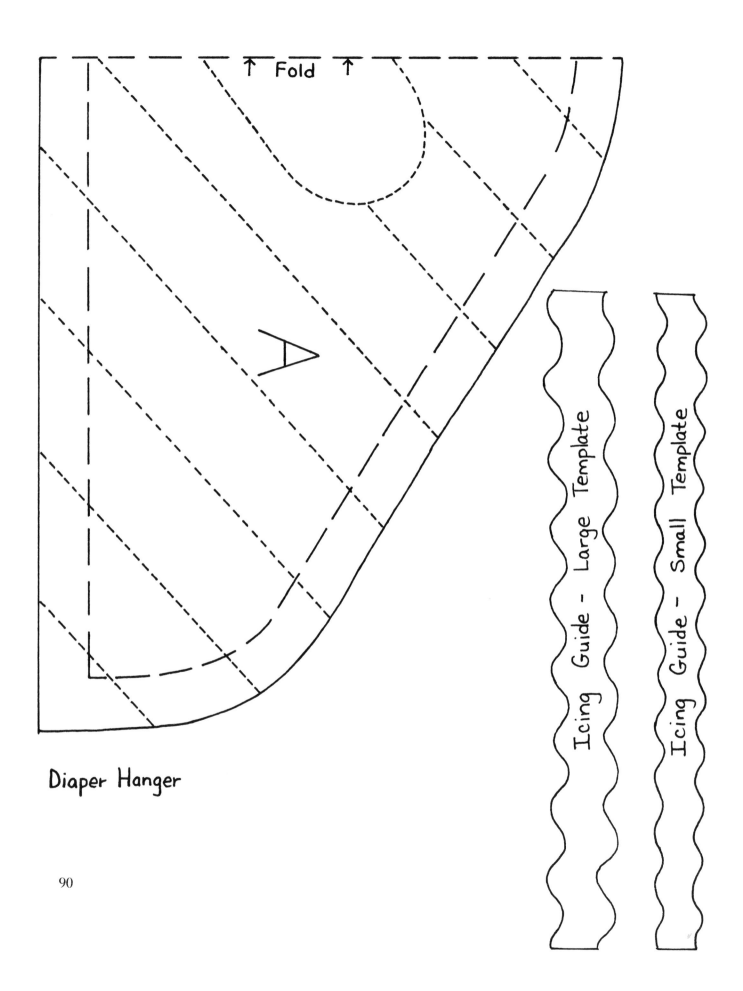

Fold

A

Diaper Hanger

Icing Guide – Large Template

Icing Guide – Small Template

90

Chapter 4

Little Red Riding Hood

Fig. 4-1
Girl's hooded jacket (front).

Fig. 4-2
Girl's hooded jacket (back).

92

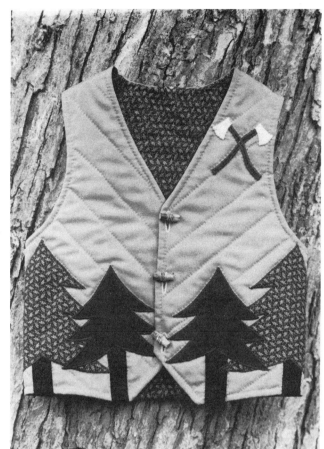

Fig. 4-3
Wolf-Woodsman vest (front).

Fig. 4-4
Wolf-Woodsman vest (back).

93

Fig. 4-5
Doll quilt or wallhanging.

Fig. 4-6
Tote bag (outside).

Fig. 4-7
Tote bag (inside).

Little Red Riding Hood and the wolf come alive on the hooded jacket, vest, and accessories presented in this chapter.

Girl's Hooded Jacket

Sew the jacket (see color section for photograph) in red and everyone will recognize this storybook favorite. It features hidden pockets—one behind a bush and one under a roof—for holding special treasures or warming small hands on a cold day. For ease in construction, each jacket piece is treated individually for appliqué and quilting before the jacket is assembled.

REQUIREMENTS

Commercial pattern for a simple hooded jacket with four main pattern pieces—
    front, back, sleeve, and hood
Yardage (44″ fabric):
    Red solid medium-weight fabric—check pattern requirements (jacket front,
        back, sleeves, button loops, and hood; Red Riding Hood pattern 1)
    Brown print—$\frac{3}{4}$ yd., plus pattern requirements for the lining (jacket lining,
        foreground scene, $1\frac{1}{4}″ \times 5$ yds. for bias binding
    Dark-green solid—$\frac{1}{3}$ yd. (trees)
    Medium-green print—$\frac{1}{3}$ yd. (trees)
    Assorted fabric scraps (remaining appliqués, pockets, and button loops)
    Fleece or traditional batting—same as for red solid
    Lightweight fusible interfacing—$\frac{1}{2}$ yd.
Red quilting thread
Coordinated thread for machine appliqué and sewing
Six-strand embroidery floss for details on wolf
Buttons—see pattern requirements

DIRECTIONS

1. Cut from fabric, lining, and batting all pieces needed to construct the jacket. Make the lining $\frac{1}{8}″$ larger all the way around in order to accommodate quilting.
2. Cut brown foreground print 6″ wide for the jacket bottom and 4″ wide for the sleeves. The other dimensions will depend on the pattern size.
3. Mark the placement line for the foreground on the jacket sleeves and bottom. Match the placement and stitching line and sew the foreground to the jacket pieces, right sides together (Fig. 4-8). Trim the side edges of the foreground to match the jacket pieces.
4. Cut all appliqués from fabric that has been fused to interfacing. Cut Red Riding Hood (pattern 1) from the red solid and 11 tree trunks and the wolf from scrap fabric. From the dark-green solid, cut one tree from pattern B and four trees from pattern D. From the medium-green print, cut two trees from pattern A and four trees from pattern C.
5. Using a glue stick or pins, position the fused appliqués on the jacket pieces

and machine appliqué. Sew the pieces in the following order: trunks, trees, Red Riding Hood, and wolf (without the bush) (Fig. 4-9).

6. Embroider details on the wolf's face.

7. Add $\frac{1}{2}''$ seam allowance to house, roof, and bush templates. Cut from the fabric scraps one door and two each of house, roof, windows, and bush. With right sides together, sew the matching pieces together almost all the way around, leaving a small opening at the bottom for turning. Trim the seams and clip the curves. Turn and press. Appliqué the door and windows on the house. Topstitch the roof and house (Fig. 4-10).

8. Double stitch the roof, house, and bush in place (Fig. 4-11). The double stitching is attractive and also makes the pocket more durable.

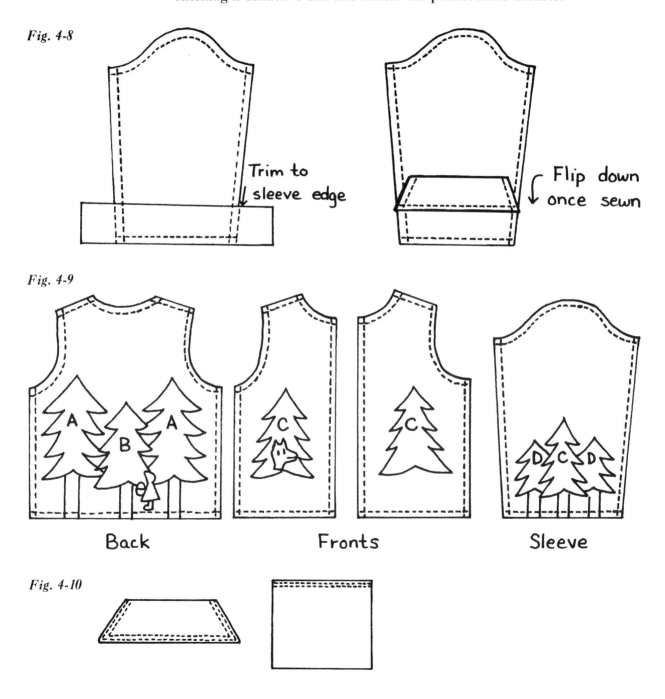

Fig. 4-8

Trim to sleeve edge

Flip down once sewn

Fig. 4-9

Back   Fronts   Sleeve

Fig. 4-10

Fig. 4-11

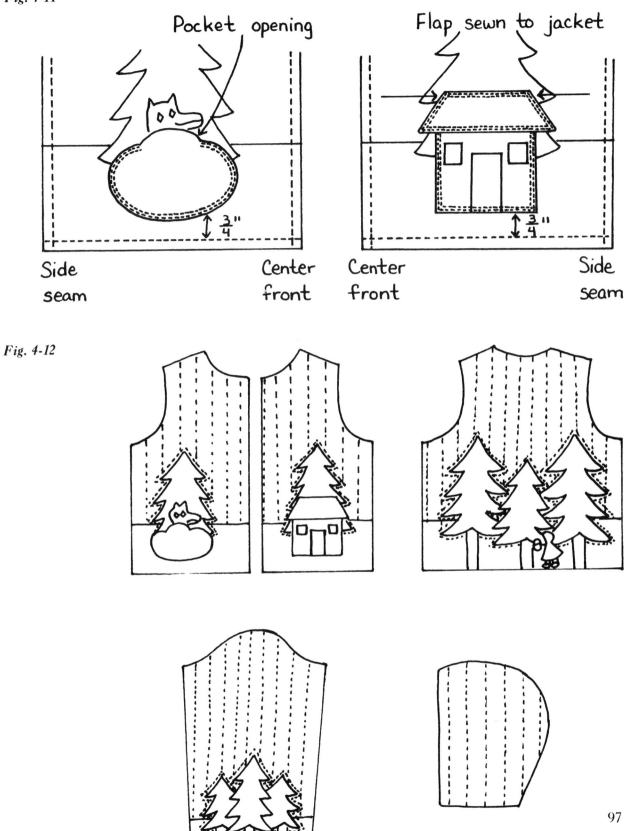

Pocket opening

Flap sewn to jacket

$\frac{3}{4}$"

$\frac{3}{4}$"

Side
seam

Center
front

Center
front

Side
seam

Fig. 4-12

97

Fig. 4-13

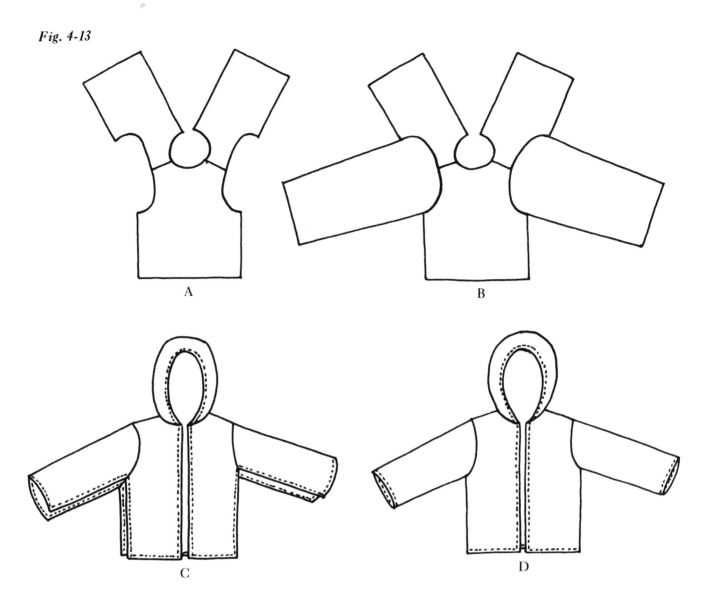

A

B

C

D

Fig. 4-14

Trim this side to ¼"

$\frac{5}{8}$" seam allowance

Fold over, encasing the raw edges, and slipstitch

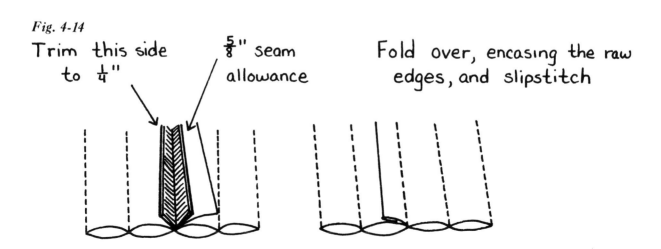

Fig. 4-15

99
*Little Red
Riding Hood*

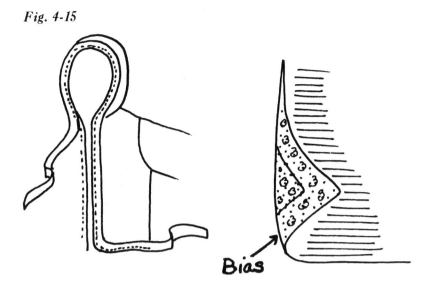

Bias

9. To make quilting easier, carefully trim the excess jacket fabric from behind the brown foreground, leaving $\frac{1}{4}''$ seam allowances.

10. Following the suggested quilting lines (Fig. 4-12) for each jacket piece, mark the lines with a ruler and a water-soluble marker or pencil. Mark the vertical quilting lines, spacing them $1\frac{1}{2}''$ apart. Layer the jacket piece, fleece, and lining, and baste together. Machine or hand quilt with matching thread. Quilt around the edges of all shapes and again $\frac{1}{4}''$ from the edges of the trees (Fig. 4-12).

11. Assemble the jacket according to pattern instructions using the $\frac{5}{8}''$ seam allowance called for. Finish the seams after each step. This is usually done in the following order: shoulder seams, sleeve to jacket, hood to neck, and sleeves and sides (Fig. 4-13). To finish the seams, trim one seam to $\frac{1}{4}''$ and overlap with the other. Hand stitch in place (Fig. 4-14).

12. Using a strip of fabric $1'' \times 8''$ long, make button loops (see instructions in Chapter 1). Sew completed loops to the jacket front.

13. Make a continuous bias of the remaining brown-foreground fabric (see instructions in Chapter 1). With right sides together, sew the bias to all raw edges on the jacket and sleeves. Fold the seams and bias to the inside of the jacket so that no trim can be seen on the front (Fig. 4-15).

14. Complete the jacket by sewing on the buttons.

Wolf-Woodsman Vest

As a companion to the Red Riding Hood jacket, this vest (see color section for photograph) features the kind of scary creature little boys delight in. Make the wolf from terry or a napped fabric so that the garment will have a tactile as well as visual effect.

REQUIREMENTS

Commercial pattern in child's size—one back and one front piece (no darts, princess lines, or lapels)

Yardage (44″ fabric):

Tan solid—$\frac{1}{2}$ to $\frac{3}{4}$ yd; check pattern requirements (vest back and front)

Medium-green print—$\frac{3}{4}$ to 1 yd. (vest lining and trees)

Dark-green solid—$\frac{1}{4}$ yd. (trees)

Light-tan print—$\frac{1}{4}$ yd. (wolf background and ax heads)

Black terry—$\frac{1}{4}$ yd. (wolf head)

Assorted fabric scraps (remaining appliqués)

Fleece—same as for tan solid

Lightweight fusible interfacing—$\frac{1}{2}$ yd.

Quilting thread

Coordinated thread for sewing and machine appliqué

Sheet of medium-weight paper measuring at least $8\frac{1}{2}″ \times 11″$

Buttons

DIRECTIONS

1. Adapt vest pattern (see Chapter 1) and cut out vest, lining, and batting.

2. Position a sheet of paper over the vest back to make a pattern for the wolf background (Fig. 4-16). Trim to fit the vest back and armholes evenly.

3. Cut the wolf background square and place it in a diamond position on the vest back. Place $\frac{3}{4}″$-wide strips over the square edges and appliqué in place (Fig. 4-17). (The narrow strips on this vest can be made from a straight-grain stripe or simply from commercial bias. Machine or hand appliqué.)

4. Cut all appliqués from fabric that has been fused to interfacing. From the medium-green print, cut two trees from pattern C and one tree from pattern D. From the dark-green solid, cut two trees from pattern B and two trees from pattern D. Cut seven tree trunks, the wolf, and two axes.

Fig. 4-16

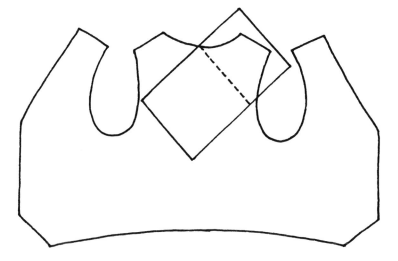

5. Position the trees and trunks on vest with pins or a glue stick, and satin stitch the edges. Before appliquéing the wolf to the vest back, make the pupils of the wolf's eyes by varying the width of the satin stitch from narrow to wide to narrow again. Position and satin stitch the wolf and axes (Fig. 4-18).
6. Trim the vest fabric from behind the wolf inset to reduce bulk and make quilting easier.
7. Leaving shoulder seams open, sew the vest, lining, and fleece together, laying the vest and lining right sides together with the fleece on top (Fig. 4-19).
8. Trim seams, clip curves, and turn the vest through the shoulder openings.
9. Mark the quilting lines on the vest with a water-soluble marker or pencil. Use a ruler and the back inset as a guide (Fig. 4-20).

Fig. 4-17

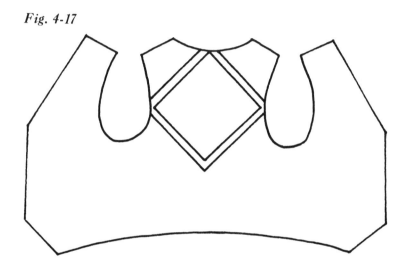

Fig. 4-18

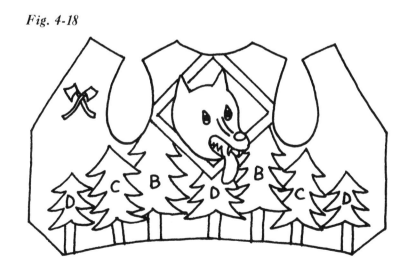

Fig. 4-19

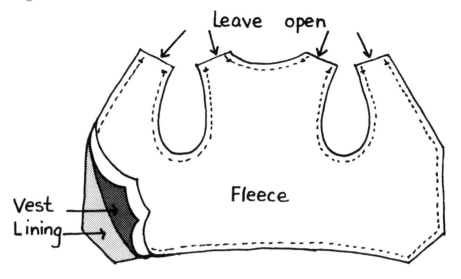

Fig. 4-20

10. Join the shoulder seams by hand using small stitches and sewing securely. Trim the batting away from the seam allowances. Slipstitch lining closed.
11. Quilt the vest with matching thread. Any heavy thread or buttonhole twist coated with beeswax will work if matching quilting thread cannot be found.
12. Make the buttonholes and sew on the buttons to finish.

Doll Quilt or Wallhanging

Make this small quilt (see color section for photograph) for a special doll, or use it to set a theme in a little girl's room. The 21″ square quilt has an appliquéd center surrounded by pieced trees in its border. Tree trunks are appliquéd to a narrow strip that is sewn to the triangle border. Appliqué can be done by hand or machine.

REQUIREMENTS

Yardage (44″ fabric):

Brown print—$\frac{1}{2}$ yd. (13$\frac{1}{2}$″ square)

Deep-red solid—$\frac{1}{2}$ yd. (four strips 1$\frac{5}{8}$″ × 15$\frac{3}{4}$″, four strips 1$\frac{5}{8}$″ × 24$\frac{1}{2}$″, four straight-grain binding strips 1$\frac{1}{2}$″ × 26″, Red Riding Hood pattern 1)

Dark-green print—$\frac{1}{3}$ yd. (tree and 16 triangles from pattern E)

Light-tan print—$\frac{1}{4}$ yd. (basket and twenty triangles from pattern E)

Black solid or small print—$\frac{1}{8}$ yd. (tree trunks, door, and boot)

Batting—24″ square

Lining—$\frac{3}{4}$ yd. (24″ square)

Assorted fabric scraps (house, roof, windows, bush, and path)

Quilting thread

Coordinated thread for machine appliqué and sewing

DIRECTIONS

1. Cut out all fabric pieces and appliqués according to instructions in "Yardage" section. Cut the tree from pattern B. Cut the border triangles from pattern E. From the deep-red solid, cut Red Riding Hood pattern 1. Be sure to add $\frac{1}{4}$″ seam allowances to appliqués for hand appliqué.

2. Using the pattern pieces, mark the placement of the appliqués on the background fabric using a pencil or water-soluble marker (Fig. 4-21).

3. Slipstitch the appliqués to the background fabric, matching the seam line with the placement line. Sew the appliqués in the following order: tree, path, bush, house, roof, door, windows, boot, basket, and Red Riding Hood.

4. Piece four triangle borders, alternating dark and light triangles (Fig. 4-22).

5. Match the four 1$\frac{5}{8}$″ × 15$\frac{3}{4}$″ border strips to the triangle border and mark placement of the tree trunks (Fig. 4-23). Appliqué the tree trunks to the narrow border strip. Pin the tree-trunk border to the triangle border and stitch

Fig. 4-21

Fig. 4-22

Fig. 4-23

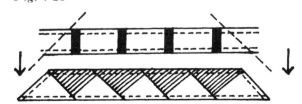

together. Stitch the borders to the background square and miter the corners (Fig. 4-24).

6. Stitch the four $1\frac{5}{8}''$ × $24\frac{1}{2}''$ strips to the outer edge of the triangle border. Miter the corners and trim the excess from the seam allowances (Fig. 4-25).

7. Press the block and mark it for quilting using a pencil or water-soluble marker (Fig. 4-26). Pin and baste the quilt top to the batting and lining. Quilt in the seam line around appliqués, border strips, and triangles as well as on the markings shown in Figure 4-26.

8. Bind the quilt with the $1\frac{1}{2}''$ × $26''$ strips, mitering the corners to finish.

9. If you intend to use this miniature quilt as a wallhanging, slipstitch a sleeve $1\frac{1}{2}''$ × $19''$ to the back of the quilt and run a dowel through it.

Fig. 4-24

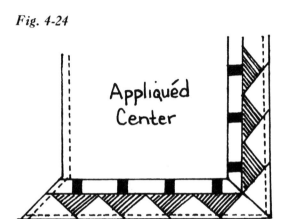

Fig. 4-25

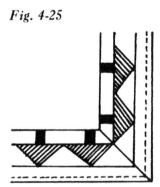

Fig. 4-26

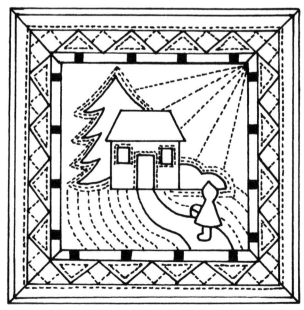

Tote Bag

This child-size storybook tote (see color section for photograph) opens on the side to show the inside of Grandma's house with the wolf in her bed. Velcro holds the two pockets together securely when the tote is carried. All appliqué is done by machine for ease in construction and durability. The finished tote bag measures $8'' \times 10\frac{1}{2}''$.

REQUIREMENTS

Yardage (44″ fabric):

Deep-red solid—$\frac{3}{4}$ yd. (18″ × 22″ rectangle, $1\frac{1}{2}''$ × 34″ facing strip, two strips 3″ × 20″ for straps, Red Riding Hood pattern 1 reverse, Red Riding Hood pattern 2)

Medium-green print—$\frac{3}{4}$ yd. (20″ × 24″ rectangle for lining and rug)

Dark-green print—$\frac{1}{4}$ yd. (trees)

Brown print—$\frac{1}{8}$ yd. ($3\frac{1}{2}''$ × 18″ rectangle for outside foreground)

Yellow stripe—$\frac{1}{4}$ yd. (two $5\frac{3}{4}''$ × $7\frac{1}{4}''$ rectangles for wallpaper)

Assorted fabric scraps (remaining appliqués)

Lightweight fusible interfacing—$\frac{1}{2}$ yd.

Fleece or needlepunch batting—19″ × 21″

Coordinated thread for machine appliqué and sewing

Quilting thread

Six-strand embroidery floss for details on sampler and wolf Velcro strip—$\frac{3}{4}''$ × $4\frac{1}{2}''$

DIRECTIONS

1. Cut out all fabric pieces according to instructions in "Yardage" section. From the deep-red solid, cut one Red Riding Hood from pattern 2 and one reverse

Fig. 4-27

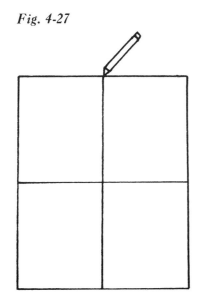

Fig. 4-28

from pattern 1. From the dark-green print, cut two trees from pattern B. Fuse the appliqués and interfacing.

2. Divide the 18″ × 22″ red fabric into quarters and mark with a pencil or water-soluble marker (Fig. 4-27).

3. Using pins or a glue stick, position the fused appliqués on the tote fabric (Fig. 4-28). Satin stitch in place. (*Note:* It is easier to do one-half of the tote bag at a time when machine appliquéing.)

4. Embroider details on the wolf's face and the letters on the "Home Sweet Home" sampler.

5. Pin and hand baste the tote to the batting and lining fabric. Hand quilt around the appliquéd scene through all layers. Do not quilt through the fused appliqués; this is too difficult to do easily, and it's not necessary when fleece or needlepunch batting is used.

6. Beginning at the center each time, machine stitch the lines marked in step 2, dividing the bag in quarters (Fig. 4-29).

7. Fold the bag in half, right sides together, and machine stitch the sides with a $\frac{5}{8}″$ seam allowance (Fig. 4-30). Trim the batting from the seams and finish them. (See Figure 4-14 for seam finishes.) Turn the bag right side out.

8. Apply the fusible interfacing to half of each strap for the tote-bag handle (Fig.

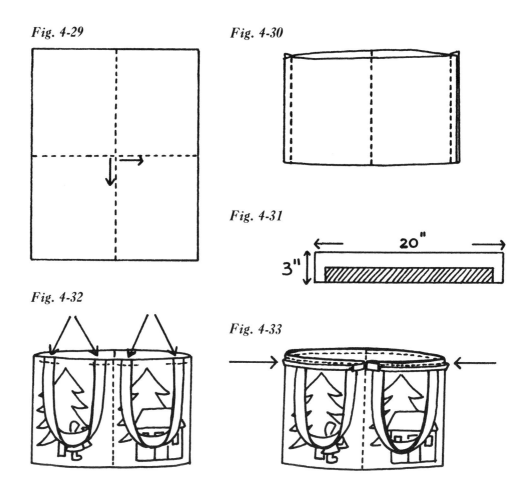

Fig. 4-29

Fig. 4-30

Fig. 4-31

Fig. 4-32

Fig. 4-33

Fig. 4-34

107
*Little Red
Riding Hood*

4-31). Sew right sides together along the lengthwise side of the straps. Trim seams, turn, and press.

9. Pin and baste the straps to the right side of the tote on the outside scene of the bag (Fig. 4-32).

10. Press one lengthwise edge of facing strip under $\frac{1}{4}''$. Right sides together, pin the unpressed edge of the facing strip to the top of the bag with raw edges even (Fig. 4-33). Machine stitch in place with $\frac{1}{2}''$ seam allowance. Trim the seam and turn the facing strip to the inside. Pin and hand or machine stitch in place. Hand stitch the Velcro in place on the edges of the inside scene to complete the bag (Fig. 4-34).

PATTERNS▶

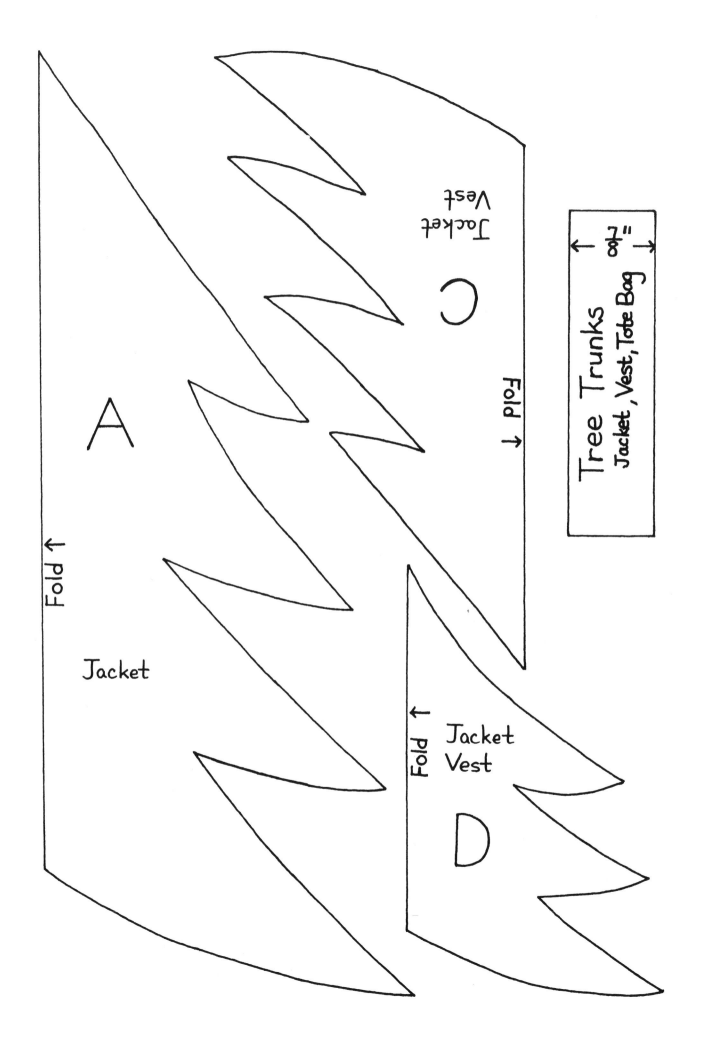

Fold ↑

A

Jacket

Tree Trunks
Jacket, Vest, Tote Bag

Jacket
Vest

Jacket
Vest

C

Fold →

D

Fold ↑

108

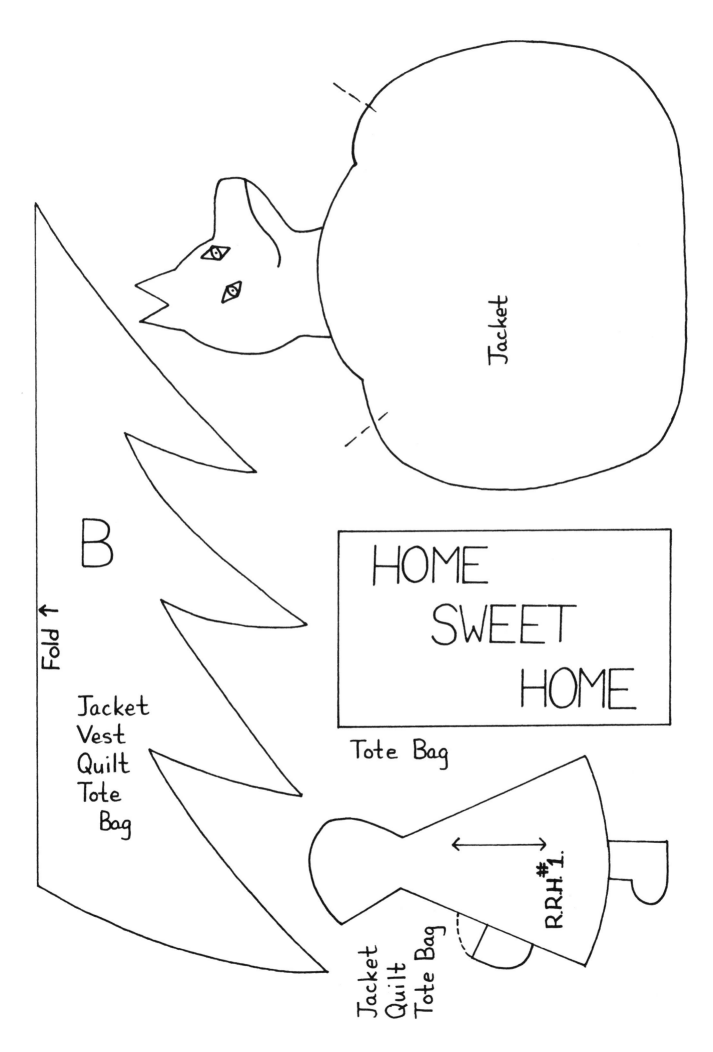

Jacket

B

Fold ↑

Jacket
Vest
Quilt
Tote
Bag

HOME
SWEET
HOME

Tote Bag

Jacket
Quilt
Tote Bag

R.R.H. #1.

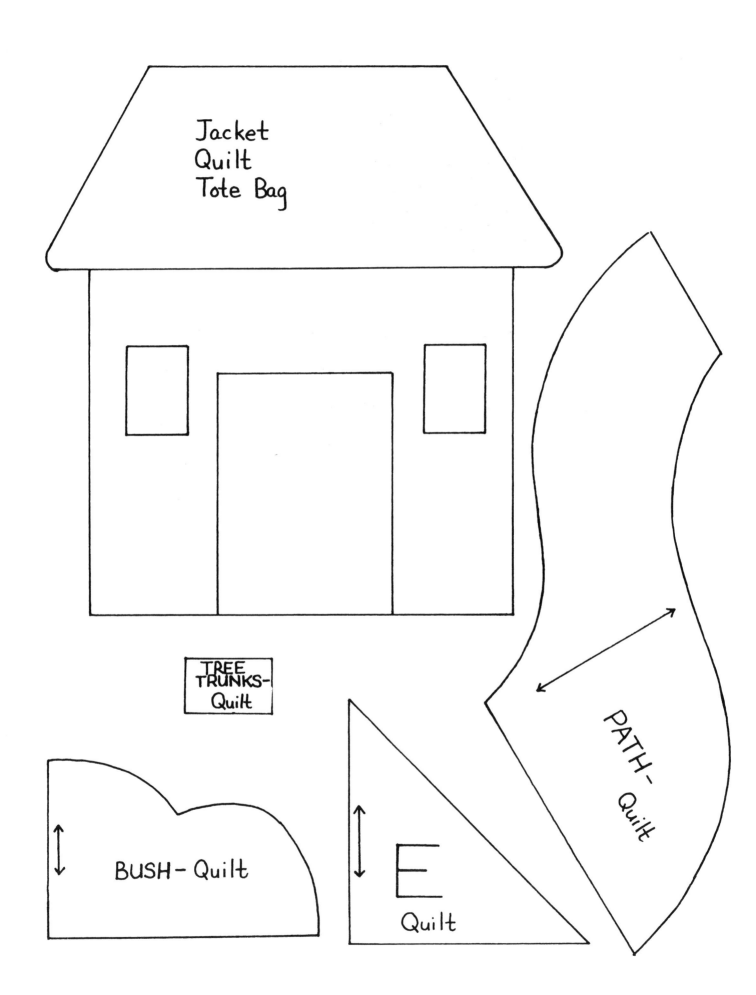

Jacket
Quilt
Tote Bag

TREE
TRUNKS-
Quilt

BUSH- Quilt

E
Quilt

PATH-
Quilt

110

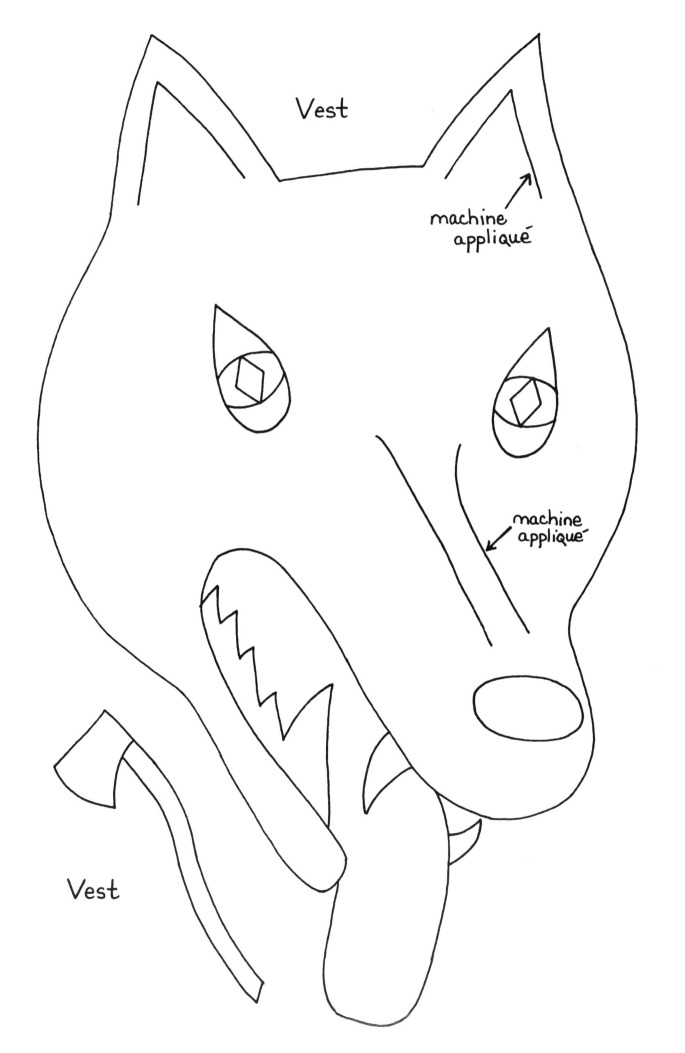

Vest

machine
appliqué

machine
appliqué

Vest

111

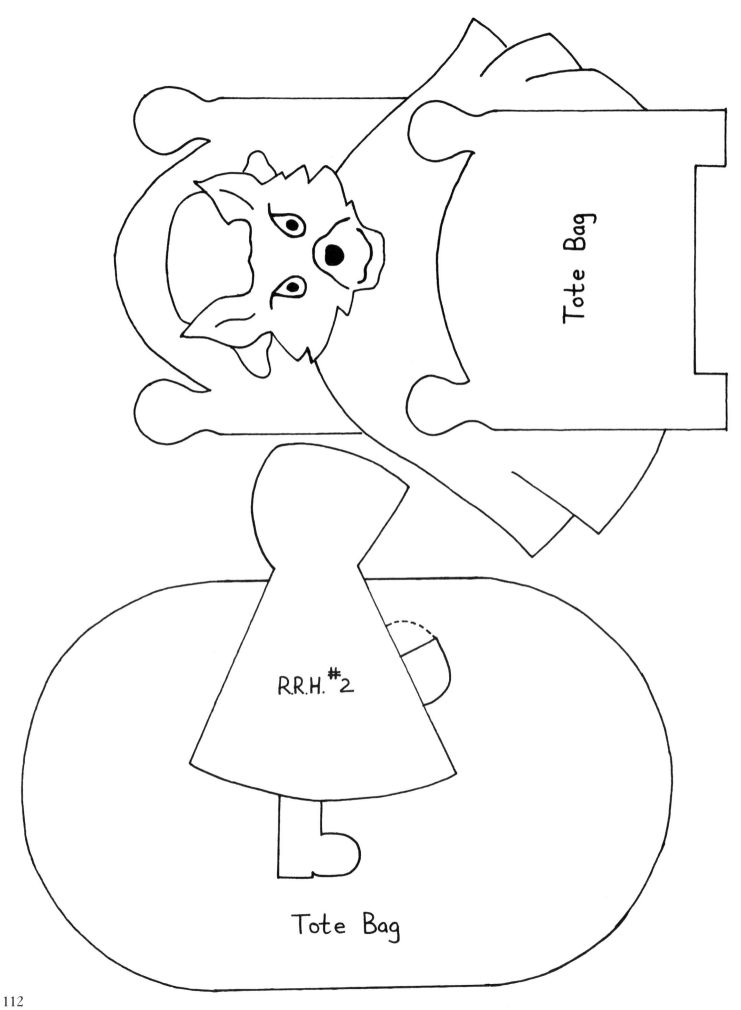

Tote Bag

R.R.H. #2

Tote Bag

Chapter 5

The Three Little Pigs

Fig. 5-1
Overalls and jumper.

Fig. 5-2
Exercise mat.

Fig. 5-3
Place mats.

You don't need a set of triplets to make the Three Little Pigs overalls, jumper, exercise mat, or place mats.

Overalls and Jumper

The appliquéd designs can be transferred to any commercial pattern or plain A-line jumper. We made our bib-front overalls from a medium-weight denim and did all the appliqué work by machine for speed, durability, and a crisp, clean look. See the color section of the book for a photograph of the overalls and jumper.

REQUIREMENTS

Commercial pattern for bib-front overalls or jumper
Yardage (44″ fabric):
    Denim or other medium-weight cotton, such as poplin, chino, drill, or pinwale
        corduroy—check pattern requirements
    Assorted fabric scraps:
      Three or four shades of green for trees and bushes
      Light-pink solid for pigs
      Yellow or gold print for straw house
      Tan or brown stripe for stick house
      Red check, gingham, or print for brick house
    Lightweight fusible interfacing—$\frac{1}{4}$ yd.
Coordinated thread for machine appliqué and sewing
Black, white, and light-rust embroidery floss (six-strand) for details on pig
Buttons or overall fasteners—see pattern requirements

DIRECTIONS

1. Cut from fabric all pieces needed to construct the overalls. Set aside all pieces except the bib front.
2. Choose style A, B, or C from Figure 5-4. (See also Figure 5-1 and the photograph in the color section to help you choose.) From the fabric scraps that have been fused to interfacing, cut appliqué piece A, B, or C. Choose different shades of green for the bushes.
3. Position the fused appliqués on the bib front and glue in place with a glue stick (Fig. 5-4). You may have to adjust the pieces slightly to fit the dimensions of the particular size bib front you are working with. Make sure you keep the appliqués at least $\frac{3}{8}$″ away from the seam-allowance markings. (This is to allow for two rows of topstitching around the outside of the bib later in the construction of the garment. See Fig. 5-5.)
4. Machine appliqué around all pieces and along the dotted lines marked on the patterns, using matching thread.
5. Embroider details on the pig. Check the patterns for details and markings.
6. Follow the commercial pattern instructions to complete the garment.
7. If you do not want your machine-appliqué work to show on the wrong side of the bib, cut a second bib front to use as a facing. Sew the right sides together, turn, and you will have a clean finish on the inside.

Fig. 5-4

Fig. 5-5

Exercise Mat

For exercising or relaxing, this portable mat (see color section for photograph) is just the thing for active little ones. All sewing is done by machine. Use a medium-weight fabric, such as kettlecloth, for the appliqué background and it will withstand plenty of hard use. The finished size of the mat is 22″ × 62″.

REQUIREMENTS

Yardage (44″ fabric):

Navy solid, such as kettlecloth or poplin—$1\frac{3}{4}$ yd. (22″ × 62″ rectangle)

Coordinating print fabric—2 yds. (24″ × 64″ rectangle for lining, two strips 4″ × 66″ for vertical borders, two strips 4″ × 26″ for horizontal borders, and four strips 3″ × 26″ for ties. (The ties will be cut in half after sewing to make eight strips.)

Solid white—9″ square (clouds)

Assorted fabric scraps for appliqués—see description under yardage for bib overalls

Fusible interfacing—2 yds.

Lightweight nonfusible interfacing—three 18″ × 20″ pieces (used as stabilizer behind navy background during machine appliqué)

High-loft batting—two 24″ × 64″ rectangles

Coordinated thread for machine appliqué and sewing

Black, white, and light-rust embroidery floss for details on pig

DIRECTIONS

1. Cut the navy background piece. Using a chalk pencil or water-soluble marker, divide the piece into three sections, as shown in Fig. 5-6.

116

2. Cut all appliqués from fabric that has been fused to interfacing. Cut the clouds from the white fabric and the other appliqués, including the reverse pieces, from the fabric scraps. (Figure 5-7 shows which appliqués to cut.)

3. Position the appliqués on the marked background and assemble the scenes using Figure 5-7 as a guide. The arrangement of trees, bushes, and houses does not have to be exactly like ours. Experiment with color and print combinations. Create your own bush and cloud shapes, if you wish. *Note:* When finishing the outside edges in a later step, you will take 1″ seam allowances, so keep all appliqués at least another inch away from this imaginary seam line.

4. Once you have arranged each scene, glue the pieces in place with a glue stick. Because of the size of the mat and the number of appliqués, you may want to secure the pieces with additional pins, tape, or large hand-basting stitches until they are all sewn. It will be easier and less time-consuming to appliqué all the clouds first, using white thread, then all the light-green prints, using light-green thread, and so on, skipping from scene to scene. This will eliminate the necessity of changing the top thread often.

5. Pin or baste the nonfusible interfacing pieces (18″ × 20″) to the wrong side of the mat behind each section to be appliquéd.

6. Follow steps 4 and 5 of the bib-front overalls directions.

Fig. 5-6

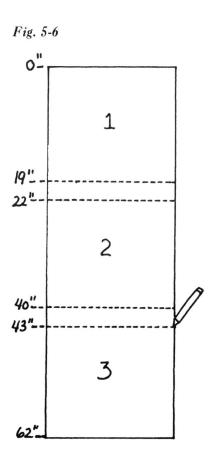

Fig. 5-7

7. On the wrong side, trim away the interfacing from the outside edges of the large appliqué areas in each section (Fig. 5-8).

8. Press the appliquéd top and smooth it out over one layer of high-loft batting. Hand baste around the edges and across the scenes to secure (Fig. 5-9).

9. Using navy thread and a straight machine stitch with 10 to 12 stitches per inch, sew around the large appliquéd areas of each scene as close as possible to the satin stitching. Remove the basting.

10. From the print fabric, cut out the lining and lay it out right side down. Place the second layer of batting on top of the lining and place the appliquéd mat on top, right side up. Pin and baste around the edges to secure all layers.

11. Machine stitch through all thicknesses along the marked lines that divide the three scenes. True the side edges of the mat, making sure they are straight. Trim the excess lining and batting to within 1″ of the seam lines, making all raw edges even.

12. Cut the vertical and horizontal border strips from the print fabric. The border strips are applied in the same way you would apply a bias edge. The only difference is that these strips are cut on the straight of grain. The finished width of the strip will be 1″. Pin the strips to the mat, allowing a 2″ excess

Fig. 5-9

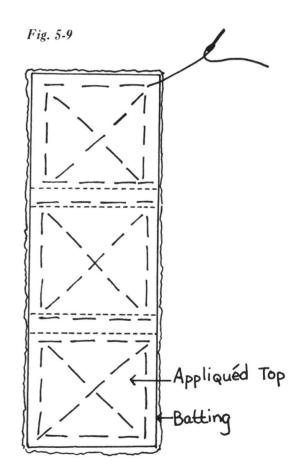

Fig. 5-8

at each corner. Sew the strips to the mat right sides together, taking a 1″ seam allowance, and start and stop the stitching 1″ from each corner (Fig. 5-10).

13. Cut the four 3″ × 26″ ties from the print fabric. Wrong sides together, press each tie in half lengthwise. Open up and fuse a strip of interfacing 1″ × 25″ to one side of each strip along the center fold on the wrong side of the fabric (Fig. 5-11). Press $\frac{1}{2}$″ seam allowances to the inside. Fold strip lengthwise, wrong sides together, topstitch close to all the edges around the ties, and cut the ties in half crosswise (Fig. 5-12).

14. See the instructions in Chapter 1 for applying binding and mitering corners. On the wrong side of the mat, tuck the raw edges of the ties underneath the 1″ border for placement (Fig. 5-13). Pin the raw edges of the binding under and slipstitch closed, or machine stitch in the seam line from the front all the way around border seam, catching the folded edge of the border on the wrong side of the mat.

15. The mat can be folded and tied when not in use.

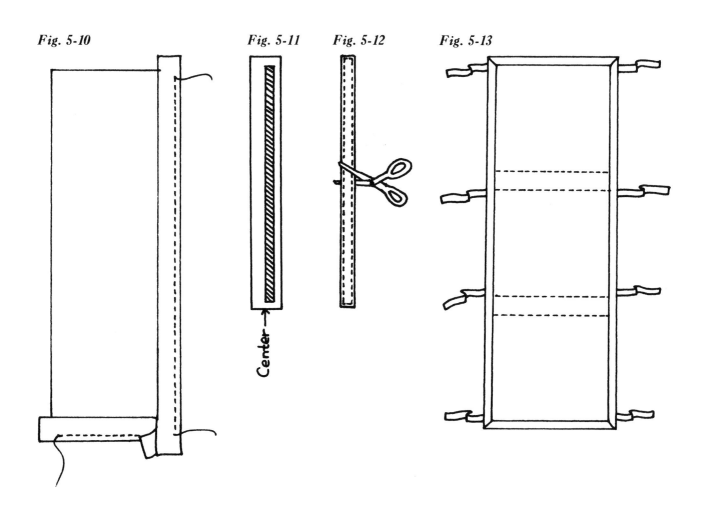

Fig. 5-10   *Fig. 5-11*   *Fig. 5-12*   *Fig. 5-13*

Place Mats

You don't have to have a party of four to enjoy these storybook place mats (see color section for photograph). Make them of durable denim or kettlecloth with machine-appliquéd figures and they will withstand much use and many launderings.

REQUIREMENTS

Yardage for set of four (44″ fabric):

Navy solid (denim or kettlecloth)—$\frac{3}{4}$ yd.

Coordinating print fabric—1 yd. (lining)

Assorted fabric scraps for appliqués—(see description under yardages for bib overalls)

Lightweight nonfusible interfacing—28″ × 38″ rectangle

Lightweight fusible interfacing—1 yd.

Fleece or needlepunch batting—1 yd.

Six-strand embroidery floss for details on pigs and wolf

Coordinated thread for machine appliqué and sewing

DIRECTIONS

1. Make a paper pattern for the place mats from a rectangle 13″ × 18½″ (Fig. 5-14). Fold in quarters and trim away the outside corners in a soft curve to form an oval when the pattern is fully opened (Fig. 5-15).
2. Layer the solid fabric, fleece, nonfusible interfacing, and lining. Then cut out four place mats through all layers, using the paper pattern.
3. Set aside the lining layers. Baste together four each of the remaining three layers (Fig. 5-16).
4. Cut the appliqués, including the reverse pieces, from the fabric scraps that have been fused to interfacing. (Figure 5-17 shows which appliqués to cut.) Position the fused appliqués on the mats and glue them in place with a glue stick. Remember that bush, tree, and cloud placement does not have to be exactly like ours. Machine appliqué with matching thread around all pieces and along the dotted lines on the patterns.

Fig. 5-14

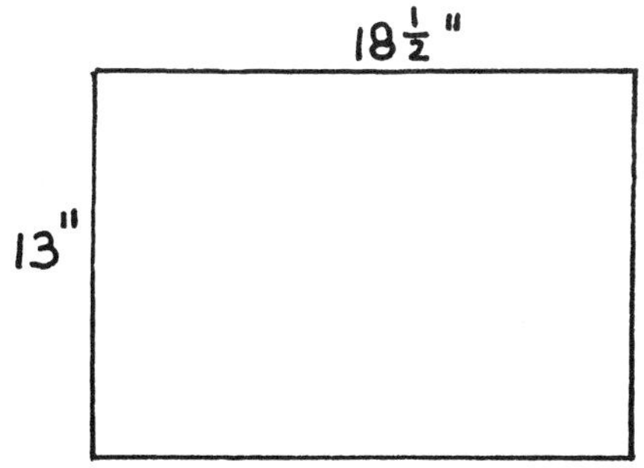

Fig. 5-15

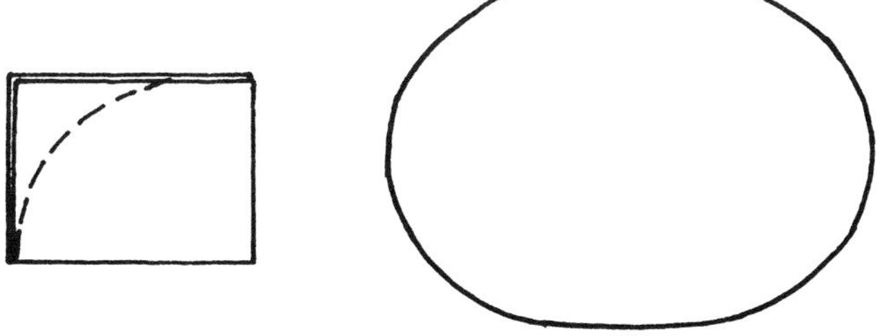

5. Trim away the nonfusible interfacing from the back side of each mat.
6. Embroider details on the pigs and wolf. Check the patterns for details and markings.
7. Pin the wrong side of the linings to the wrong side of the mats. Baste around the outside edges.
8. Mark the quilting lines and machine quilt through all thicknesses (Fig. 5-18). Top thread should match the background fabric, and bobbin thread should

Fig. 5-16

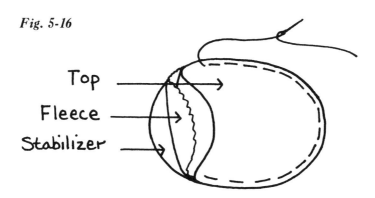

Fig. 5-17

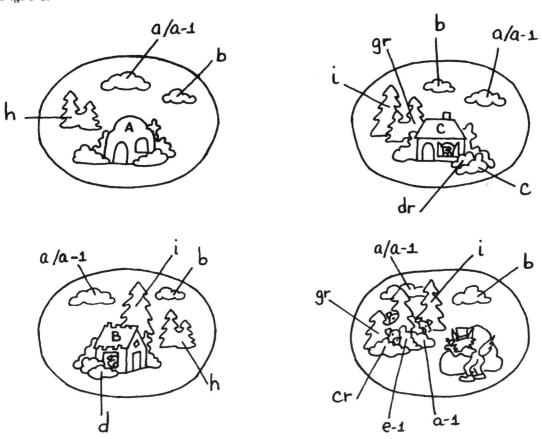

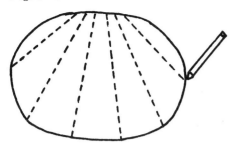

Fig. 5-18

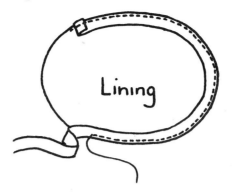

Fig. 5-19

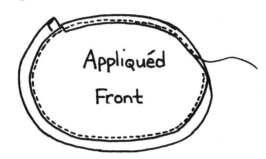

Fig. 5-20

match the lining fabric. Machine quilt around all appliqués in the seam line and along the marked lines.

9. Make a $1\frac{1}{4}''$ continuous bias from the remainder of the lining fabric according to the instructions in Chapter 1.

10. Right sides together, stitch the bias to the place mat back with a $\frac{1}{4}''$ seam allowance. Be sure to fold the bias back on itself when you begin to stitch so that you will have a clean finished edge when you fold the bias over to the front (Fig. 5-19). Fold the bias to the place mat front and fold the edge under $\frac{1}{4}''$. From the front, hand stitch in place, or machine stitch very close to the folded edge (Fig. 5-20).

PATTERNS▶

Cloud/Bush
a-1
a

Bush

Bush

Exercise Mat
Place Mats

A

Cloud b

Overalls/Jumper
Exercise Mat
Place Mats

Bush

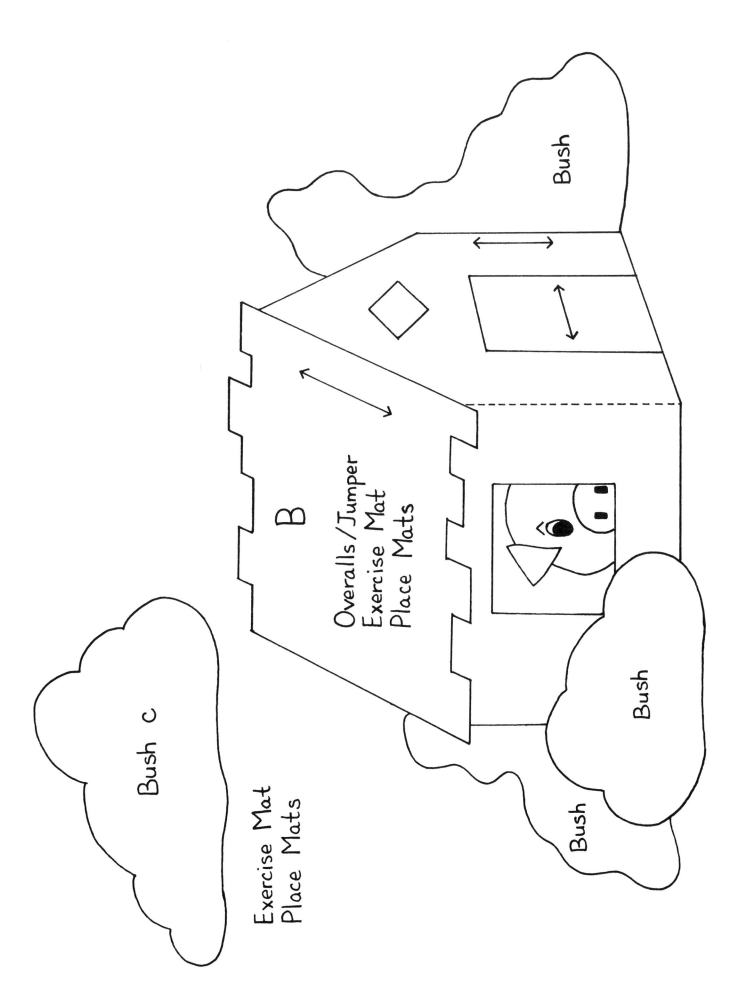

Bush

Bush

Bush

Bush c

B

Overalls / Jumper
Exercise Mat
Place Mats

Exercise Mat
Place Mats

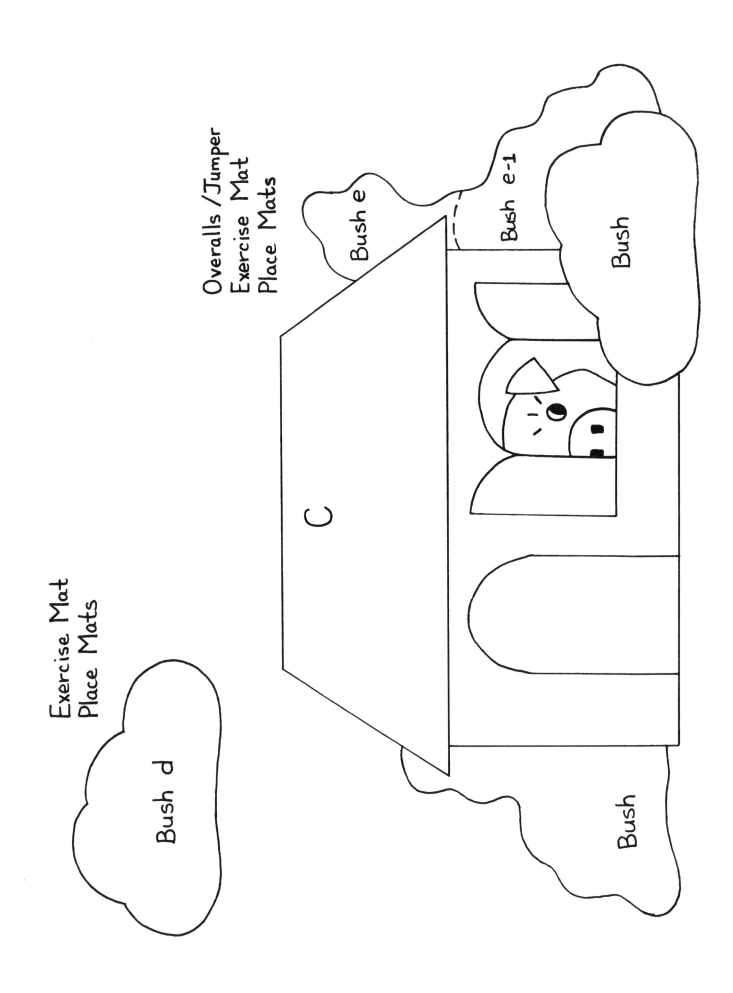

Overalls /Jumper
Exercise Mat
Place Mats

Bush e

Bush e-1

Bush

C

Exercise Mat
Place Mats

Bush d

Bush

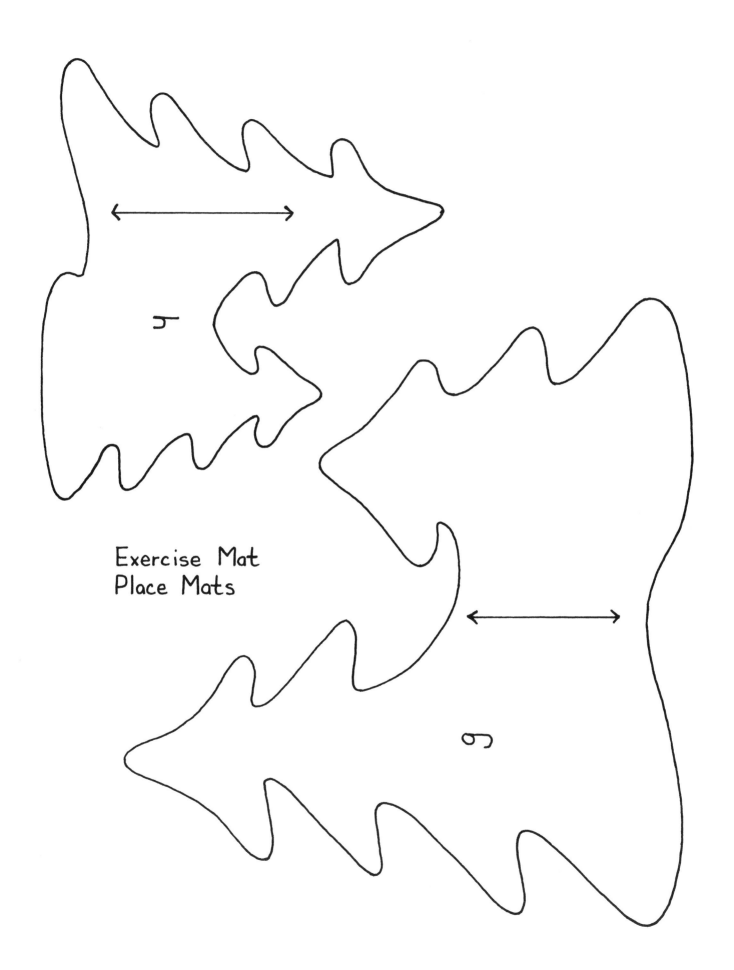

Exercise Mat
Place Mats

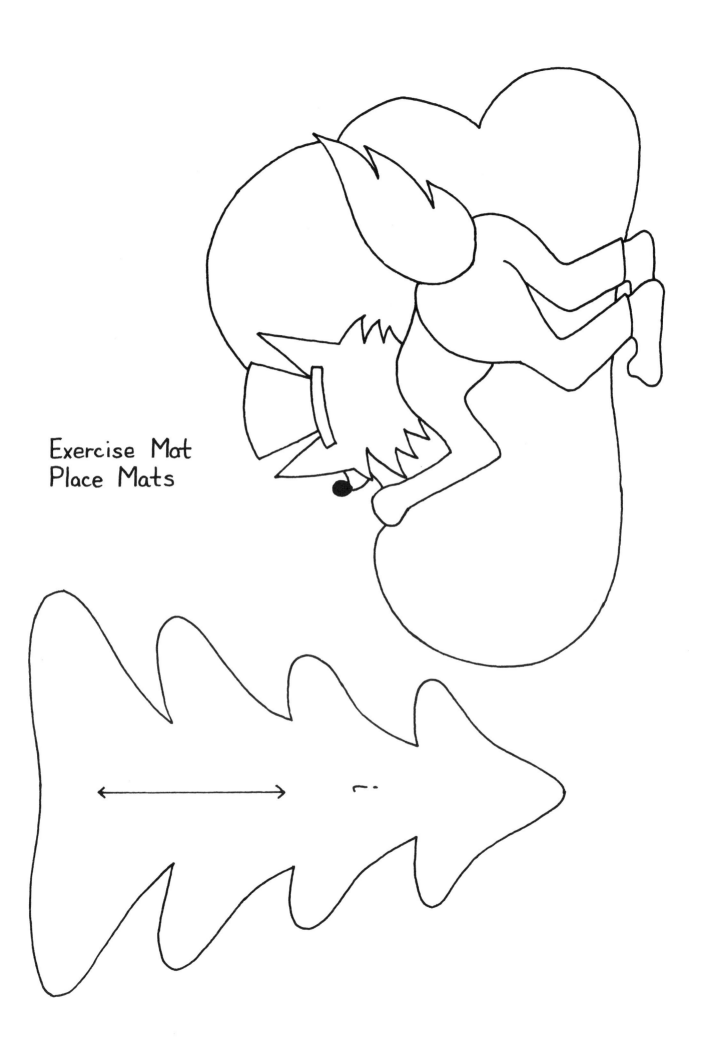

Exercise Mat
Place Mats

Chapter 6

 airy Princess Stories

A

B

Fig. 6-1
(A) "Once upon a time" quilt (B) Close-up of center medallion.

Fig. 6-2
(A) Rapunzel pinafore (B) Sleeping Beauty dress and vest (C) Cinderella bib-collar.

A   B   C

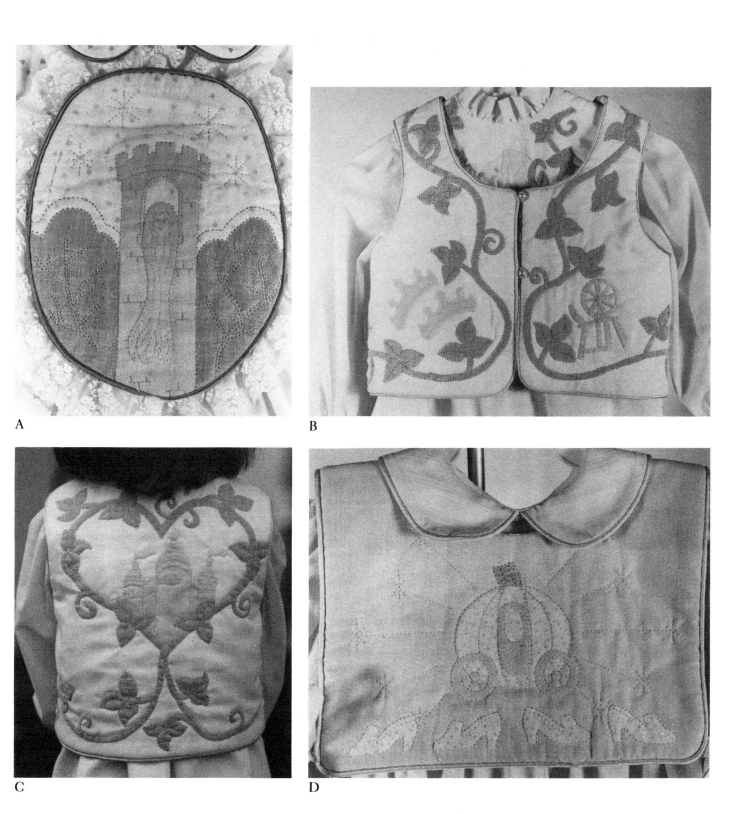

A

B

C

D

Fig. 6-3
(A) Pinafore bib front (B) Vest front (C) Vest back (D) Bib-collar front.

A B C

Fig. 6-4
Fairy princess pillows: (A) Rapunzel (*B) Sleeping Beauty (C) Cinderella.*

What little girl will not delight in dressing like Cinderella, Rapunzel, or Sleeping Beauty—in feeling like a princess?

"Once upon a Time" Quilt

Shadow appliqué, explained in Chapter 1, gives the center medallion of the "Once upon a time" quilt (see color section for photograph) a faraway, fairyland look. The 18″ × 27″ oval is quilted and then appliquéd to the quilt top. The scroll, hearts, leaves, and flower motifs are appliquéd on the quilt top, borders, and corners. Embroidery on the scroll and flowers adds a special touch. The finished quilt is 66″ by 100″ (twin-bed size).

REQUIREMENTS

Yardage (44″ fabric):

> White solid—5 yds. (large center rectangle 38″ × 74″; two outside border strips 13″ × 75½″; two outside border strips 13″ × 39½″; four 13″ corner squares; and one each of clouds in patterns W, X, and Y. Like other appliqués in center medallion, clouds must be fused to interfacing before they are cut.)
>
> Light-green solid—1 yd. (inside border strips; fourteen leaves from pattern A; and 12 yds. continuous bias 1¼″ wide)
>
> Medium-green solid—1 yd. (15″ × 20″ rectangle for medallion; fourteen leaves, pattern B; four flower parts, pattern S; two leaf patterns L1–6 without vine attached; two reverse leaf patterns L1–6 without vine; 2 yds. continuous bias 1¼″ wide for vine)
>
> Light pink—¼ yd. (seven large hearts, pattern D)
>
> Medium pink—¼ yd. (seven small hearts, pattern C)
>
> Light turquoise/blue—¼ yd. (one scroll center, pattern E; one scroll ribbon, pattern F, and one reverse)
>
> Medium turquoise/blue—scrap (one scroll piece, pattern G, and one reverse)
>
> Dark turquoise/blue—scrap (one scroll piece, pattern G-1, and one reverse)
>
> Light yellow—¼ yd. (two flowers, pattern H; four flowers, pattern J)
>
> Dark yellow—scrap (two flower centers, pattern K)
>
> Lightweight to medium-weight interfacing—1½ yds.
>
> Lining—6 yds.
>
> Batting—70″ × 104″

Center Medallion:

> White voile or batiste—⅝ yd. (20″ × 30″ rectangle)
>
> Bright blue—½ yd. (15″ × 20″ rectangle)
>
> Fuse following fabrics to interfacing before cutting:
>
> Tan or solid pindot—⅓ yd. (castle)
>
> Bright green—½ yd. (cut as one piece pattern L1–6 with vine attached, then cut one in reverse; one each of leaf patterns L-7, L-8, L-9, one each of reverse; one leaf pattern L-10; one vine, pattern M, and one reverse.)
>
> Dark brown—¼ yd. (one castle door, pattern N; one tower window, pattern O, and two small windows, pattern P; one large roof, pattern T, and two small roofs, pattern T-1)

Assorted pastel solids and pindots—(one flower and center, patterns H and
  K; two each, patterns J, Q, and R; two flowers, pattern Z; one flag,
  pattern U; two flags, pattern V)
Bright-yellow and bright-pink embroidery floss
White and different brightly colored quilting thread
Matching colored thread for machine appliqué

DIRECTIONS

1. From the white solid, cut the center rectangle, the horizontal and vertical
   strips, the four corner squares, and one each of the appliqué clouds from
   patterns W, X, and Y, following the layout in Figure 6-5.

2. Make an 18″ × 27″ oval pattern piece. If you have an oval quilt hoop this
   size, just trace around it.

3. Cut the pattern piece in half. Adding a $\frac{1}{2}$″ seam allowance all the way around
   both pieces, cut the top half of the oval from the 15″ × 20″ bright-blue
   rectangle and the bottom half from the 15″ × 20″ medium-green rectangle
   (Fig. 6-6). Sew the two pieces together with a $\frac{1}{2}$″ seam allowance. Press the
   seam open.

4. For the shadow appliqués (all those in the center medallion), fuse fabric to
   interfacing before cutting. Referring to the "Yardage" section, cut all appli-

Fig. 6-5

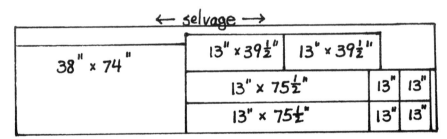

Fig. 6-6

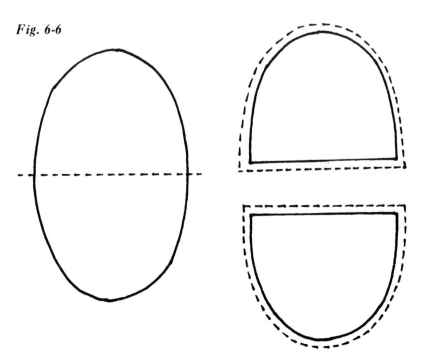

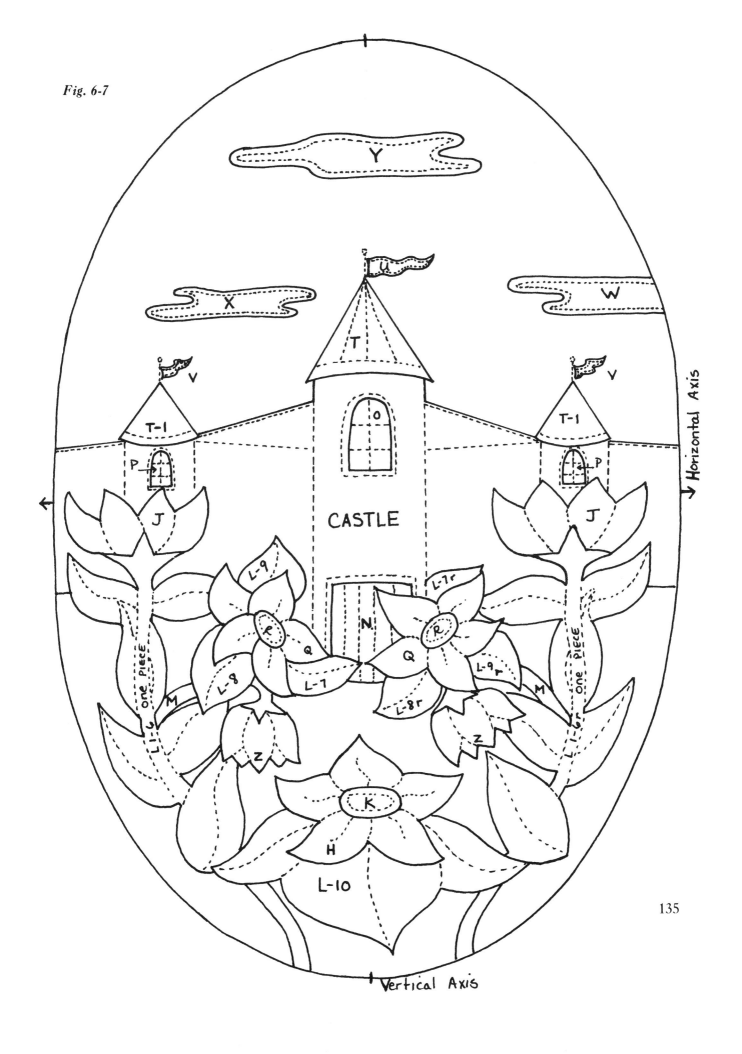

Fig. 6-7

CASTLE

135

qués exactly the same size as the patterns—leave no seam allowances. Figure 6-7 shows which appliqués to cut. Draw quilting lines on the leaves, castle, and flowers with a pencil or water-soluble marker. Make the markings just dark enough to be seen through the sheer overlay fabric.

5. Position the appliqué pieces on the blue and green oval using a glue stick or spray adhesive (Fig. 6-7). Position the castle first, matching the lines on the pattern to the vertical and horizontal axis of the oval. Then position the remaining appliqués.

6. Cut a 20″ × 30″ rectangle of sheer overlay fabric and pin it in place over the oval. (The excess can be trimmed away after quilting.)

7. Using brightly colored thread, quilt around each appliqué and along the suggested quilting lines shown on the pattern pieces and in Figure 6-7. (Quilting may be done with or without a hoop, but using a hoop makes it easier.)

8. When quilting is complete, baste the outer edges of the overlay fabric to the oval to secure. Trim excess overlay fabric.

9. Center the oval on the 38″ × 74″ rectangle. Find the center of the rectangle by folding it in quarters and creasing (Fig. 6-8). Pin and baste the center medallion in place.

10. Using a 22″ square, cut a continuous bias 12 yds. long × 1¼″ wide from the light-green fabric. (See Chapter 1.) Matching right sides to right sides, sew the bias strip in place around the medallion with a running stitch. Leave a ¼″ seam allowance. Fold the bias strip back on itself as shown in Figure 6-9. Be sure not to stretch the bias strip as you sew. When the strip is sewn in place, turn the wide portion back over the seam. Turn the raw edge under ¼″ as you go and appliqué it in place (Fig. 6-10).

Fig. 6-8

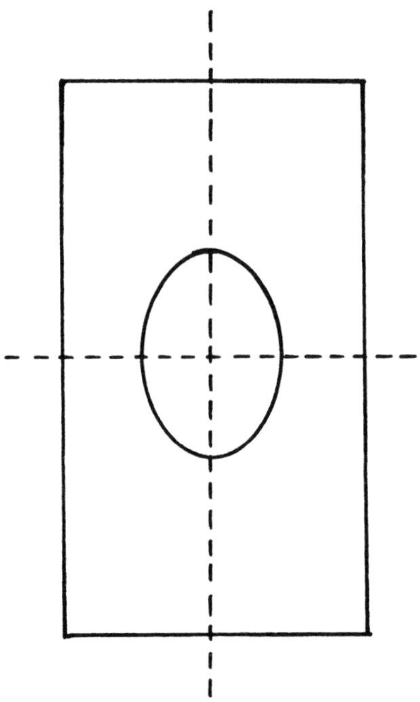

Fig. 6-9

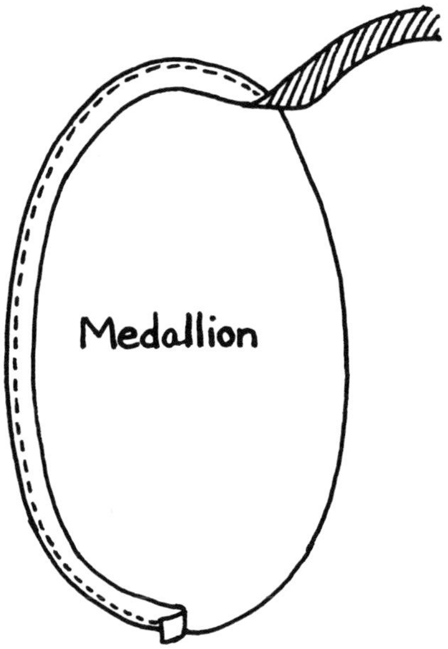

Medallion

11. Cut the rest of the appliqués and pattern pieces according to the specifications in the yardage list. Make a full-size center-scroll pattern pieice (E) and trace the letters onto it with a dark pen or marker. Place the fabric scroll piece over the pattern piece and trace the letters on the fabric with a water-soluble marker.

12. Using the appliqué pattern pieces, trace the outline of the scroll, hearts, and leaves onto the quilt top centered above and below the medallion (Fig. 6-11). Pin the appliqués in place and begin to slipstitch the matching pencil line on the appliqué to the pencil outline on the quilt top (Fig. 6-12). Embroider the letters on the scroll with three strands of bright-pink embroidery floss.

13. Using pattern pieces J, K, and H; the bright-green leaves from patterns L1–6 with vine attached; and the leaves from pattern L-10 without the vine, trace

Fig. 6-10

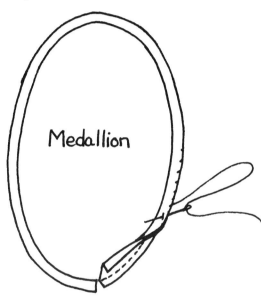

Fig. 6-11

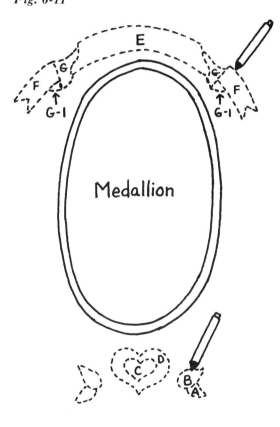

Fig. 6-12

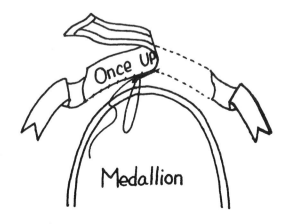

the flower and vine motif onto the quilt top at the top and bottom of the large center rectangle (Fig. 6-13). Trace the individual leaves from patterns L1–5 on the fabric and appliqué them. Next, stitch the vine in place using the same method described in Step 10. Be sure to hand sew the inside curve first. Finally, appliqué leaf pattern L-6, flowers, and flower part S. Outline the flowers using three strands of embroidery floss in a bright color (Fig. 6-14).

14. Continue in the same manner, marking and appliquéing the heart and leaf motif on the long borders and corners (Fig. 6-15).

15. Trim the background fabric from behind the scroll and medallion, leaving a $\frac{1}{4}''$ seam allowance on all edges. (Trimming this fabric will make quilting easier.)

16. From the light-green solid, cut four strips $1\frac{1}{4}'' \times 37\frac{1}{4}''$ and two strips $1\frac{1}{4}'' \times 39\frac{1}{2}''$. Sew two $1\frac{1}{4}'' \times 37\frac{1}{4}''$ strips together to make one long strip $1\frac{1}{4}'' \times 74''$. Repeat with the other two strips of the same measurements. Referring to Figure 6-16, attach the borders to the center rectangle (with $\frac{1}{4}''$ seam allowances) in the following order: (1) long narrow borders, (2) short narrow borders, (3) long wide borders, and (4) short wide borders with corners attached.

Fig. 6-13

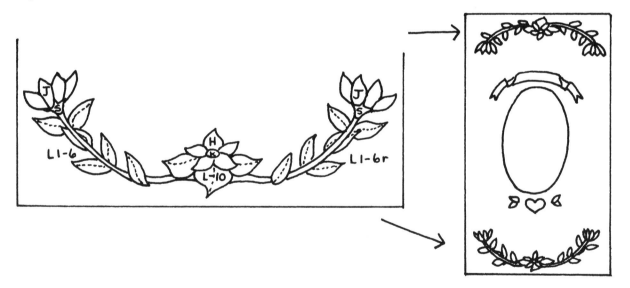

Fig. 6-14

Embroider outline and details

Fig. 6-15

139
*Fairy Princess
Stories*

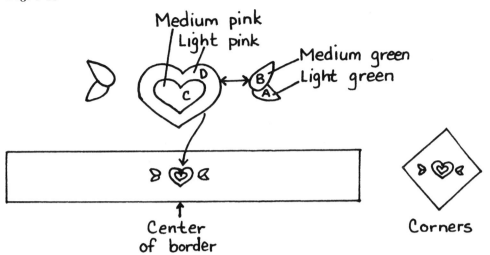

Medium pink
Light pink
Medium green
Light green

Center
of border

Corners

Fig. 6-16

4

2

3

1

1

3

$75\frac{1}{2}$"

2

39"

13"

4

13"

Fig. 6-17

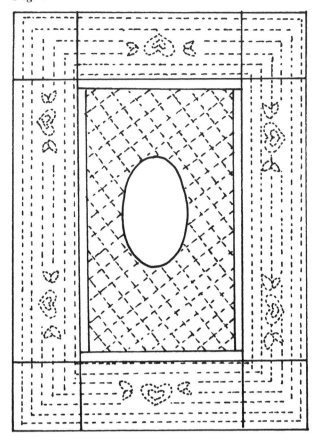

Fig. 6-18

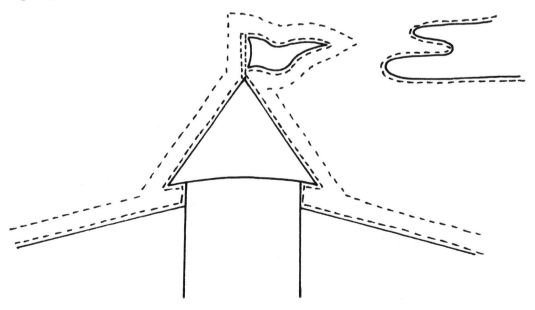

17. Press the completed quilt top. Prepare for quilting by marking very lightly with a pencil or water-soluble marker. Use the appliqué pattern pieces from the hearts and leaves to make the heart and leaf quilting design. Space evenly around the quilt borders (Fig. 6-17). Appliqués outside the medallion should be marked and quilted $\frac{1}{4}''$ in from the edge of the appliqué, in the seam lines, and $\frac{1}{4}''$ outside the seam lines for emphasis. The quilt top is marked with a latticework design that can be made by using a standard yardstick. The borders are marked and quilted with horizontal lines that meet at the corners to "frame" the quilt center. Quilting in the center medallion is limited to areas directly around the shadow appliqués, with just a small amount of quilting through the castle to reduce fullness and hold it in place. This quilting should be done with white thread on or right next to the shadow-quilting lines that define the castle sections (Fig. 6-18).

18. When quilting is finished, bind the quilt with the remainder of the light-green binding.

Sleeping Beauty Dress and Vest

Shadow appliqués and hand stitching give a soft, quilted look to this dress and vest (see color section for photograph). Its delicate quality is sure to appeal to any would-be fairy princess.

REQUIREMENTS

Commercial dress pattern in child's size with round or square yoke
Commercial vest pattern in child's size—one back and one front piece; no darts, princess lines, or lapels
Yardage for dress yoke and vest (44″ fabric):*
   White background fabric—$\frac{3}{4}$ to 1 yd. (check pattern requirements)
   White voile or batiste—same as for background fabric
   Fleece—same as for background fabric
   Bright green—$\frac{1}{2}$ yd. (leaves, vine, and tendrils)
   Bright pink—$\frac{1}{4}$ yd. (castle, crown, and face)
   Bright yellow—scrap (hair, flags, and windows)
   Bright turquoise/blue—scrap (rooftops and spinning wheel)
   White broadcloth—same as for background fabric (use lightweight; poly/cotton blend for lining)
   Fusible interfacing—1 yd.
Pink satin cording—4 to 5 yds., depending on garment size
Black and red embroidery floss for details on face
Quilting or sewing thread in deep shades of green, pink, yellow, and turquoise/blue
White thread for dress and vest construction
Buttons—two pearllike buttons for vest
*Check commercial pattern for additional fabric yardages and notions for dress.

DIRECTIONS

1. Adapt the commercial vest pattern according to the instructions in Chapter 1. Unless you can find a pattern with a scooped neck, you will also want to make some adjustments to the vest front. Measure the depth of the dress yoke (Fig. 6-19). Alter the vest front so that the neckline matches the dress yoke, allowing the yoke design to be seen (Fig. 6-20). Also remove any center-front extensions on the pattern so that the new vest front will not overlap but simply butt at the center front. Once you have completed the side, center-front, and neckline alterations, cut out the lining, foundation fabric, batting, and sheer overlay for the vest and dress yoke.

2. Vine, leaves, and heart must be adjusted to garment size. After studying Figure 6-21, make a paper-pattern heart and vine $\frac{1}{4}''$ wide to fit the vest and

Fig. 6-19

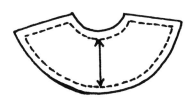

Fig. 6-20

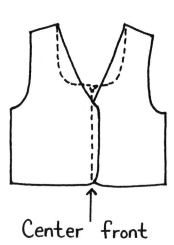

Center front

Fig. 6-21

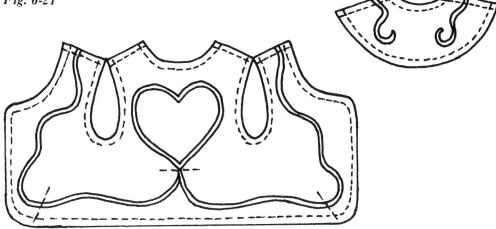

dress yoke. Remember, you need to make only half of the entire vine because it can be reversed for the opposite side of the vest and dress yoke. Once you have adjusted the pattern, use it to cut the vine and heart from green fabric that has been fused to the interfacing. It is easier to divide the vine into sections for cutting as shown by the dashed lines in Figure 6-21. If you allow a little for overlap when cutting, the piecing will not show when quilted.

3. Cut out the remainder of the shadow appliqués from the fused fabric. Refer to Figure 6-22 to determine how many of each leaf to cut. Cut out a few more leaves and tendrils than you will need so that you can experiment in arranging them on the vest. Use Figure 6-22 as a guide, but keep in mind that the arrangement will vary according to vest size. Use a pencil to mark the appliqués with quilting lines just dark enough to be seen through sheer fabric.

4. Using a glue stick or spray adhesive, position the appliqués on the background fabric.

5. Embroider the details on Sleeping Beauty's face.

6. Pin batting, background, and sheer overlay together securely. Baste through all layers around the outer edges of the vest and dress yoke. Using a dark-colored sewing or quilting thread, quilt through all layers around the outside of each appliqué and on the suggested quilting lines (see Fig. 6-3B and C).

Fig. 6-22

Quilting through the appliqués is important to prevent shifting, so you may want to do this quilting first—before you quilt around the appliqués. If shifting is a problem, pin the appliqués in place through all layers and remove the pins as you quilt.

7. Although the back of the dress yoke does not have an appliqué insert, it also needs to be quilted for a uniform appearance. Quilt through the batting, foundation, and sheer overlay (Fig. 6-23).

8. Machine baste the cording around the edges of the vest and dress yoke (Fig. 6-24). The raw edges of the cording match the raw edges of the garments.

9. To make loop buttonholes from satin cording, carefully remove the stitching from six inches of cording and discard the cord. Open the strip and press flat. Fold the raw lengthwise edges to the center and press once more. Fold again and stitch through the folded edges (Fig. 6-25). Cut the strip in half and make two soft-loop buttonholes as described in Chapter 1. Baste in place on the vest front, loops in and raw edges toward the vest edge.

10. Right sides to right sides, pin the vest lining in place. Using the basting line for the cording as a guide, machine stitch around the outer edges of the vest, leaving the shoulder seams open. Trim seams, clip curves, and turn the vest through one of the shoulder openings (Fig. 6-26).

Fig. 6-23

Fig. 6-24

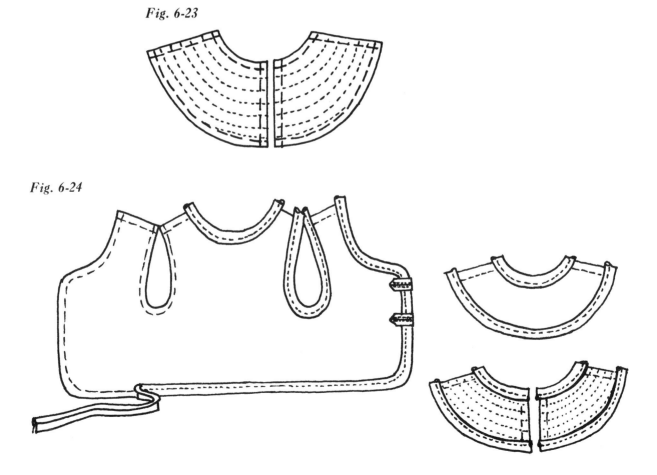

Fig. 6-25

145
*Fairy Princess
Stories*

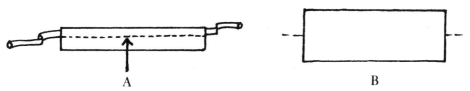

Fig. 6-26

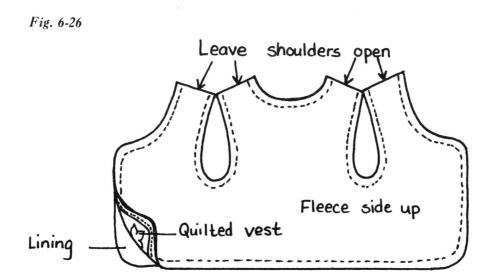

Dress: The lining for the dress yoke will probably be called the "facing" in the pattern directions. Apply this facing to the quilted dress yoke as called for in the dress pattern instructions. Complete dress according to pattern instructions.

11. With right sides together, join the shoulder seams by hand with small stitches. On the inside, slipstitch the lining at the shoulder seams. Press the shoulder seams and vest edges lightly.

12. Sew on buttons to complete.

Cinderella Bib-Collar

The Cinderella bib-collar (see color section for photograph) is designed to fit over a dress with an empire waistline. It is a good idea to choose the dress and dress fabric at the same time as or before choosing the collar fabric. Don't be afraid to try a soft stripe or print for the dress. Use a bright turquoise or blue for the background fabric of the bib-collar to re-create the enchantment of Cinderella's magical evening.

REQUIREMENTS

Yardage (44″ fabric):

Turquoise/blue background fabric—$\frac{1}{2}$ yd.

White voile or batiste—$\frac{1}{2}$ yd.

Fleece—$\frac{1}{2}$ yd.

White broadcloth (poly/cotton) for lining—$\frac{1}{2}$ yd.

Fusible interfacing—$\frac{1}{4}$ yd.

Pink and blue print (small, consistent design)—scrap (pumpkin and slippers)

Bright-pink pindot—scrap (door and wheels)

Bright green—scrap (pumpkin stem)

Pink satin cording—2 to 3 yds. (If you are making the dress, purchase enough for the collars and cuffs as well.)

Pink ribbon $\frac{3}{4}$″ wide—$2\frac{1}{2}$ yds.

Pink ribbon ($\frac{1}{4}$″ wide)—1 yd.

Bright-pink and bright-green quilting thread

Coordinated thread for appliqué and sewing

DIRECTIONS

1. Measure the bodice front and back of the dress pattern or the finished dress that will be worn with the bib-collar to determine desired length (Fig. 6-27). Be careful not to include the seam allowances when you measure the dress pattern. Also measure from armhole to armhole directly under the neck edge to determine the bib-collar width. Make a rectangular paper pattern from these measurements and add a $\frac{1}{2}$″ seam allowance (Fig. 6-28). Fold the paper in half lengthwise and crosswise to find the center and divide it into quarters. Unfold and lay flat.

2. There are two ways to determine the size of the neck opening. The easiest way is to pin the front and back bodice pattern pieces together at the shoulder and center them over the paper rectangle, matching the shoulder seams with the crosswise lines (Fig. 6-29). Trace the neck opening onto the rectangle. Enlarge the neck opening by 1″ to eliminate the neckline seam allowance and add a little ease. This line will be the cutting line for the fabric. To complete the pattern, cut in on the back bodice center line and cut out the neck hole for the bib-collar pattern (Fig. 6-30).

   You must use a different method for a ready-made dress when the pattern is not available. Use the same paper rectangle pattern divided into quarters. Measure from the center of the bodice edge to the center of the neck edge in front and back. Also measure from the shoulder edge to the neck edge on both sides. Record these distances and measure in the same amount on each of the corresponding lines on the rectangle pattern (Fig. 6-31). Connect these four points with a curving line to form the neck opening. As described in the first method, cut in on the center line of the back bodice and cut out the center opening to complete the bib-collar pattern.

3. Using this pattern, cut the bib-collar from the lining fabric, batting, blue background, and sheer overlay. Also cut the appliqués from the fused fabrics.

Fig. 6-27

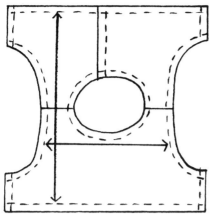

A. Using a pattern

B. Using a finished dress

Fig. 6-28

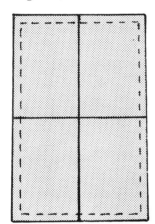

Fig. 6-29

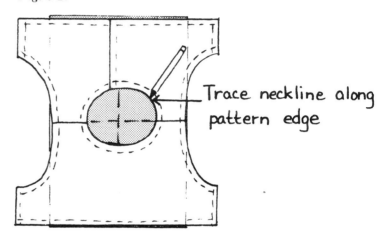

Trace neckline along pattern edge

Fig. 6-30

Cut open along center-back fold

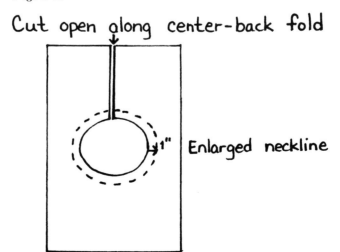

1" Enlarged neckline

Mark the quilting lines on the appliqués with a pencil, checking to make sure that they are visible through the sheer fabric.

4. Position the appliqués on the background fabric using a glue stick or spray adhesive (Fig. 6-32).

5. Sandwich the background fabric between the batting and sheer overlay and pin together securely. Baste through all layers around all edges. Mark "rays"

Fig. 6-31

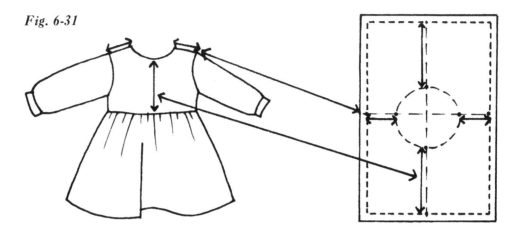

Fig. 6-32

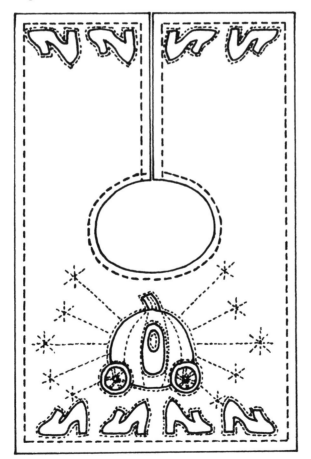

and "sparkles" on sheer overlay with a water-soluble marker. (Marks will disappear later when washed.)

6. Using the pink and green thread, quilt through and around all appliqués on the suggested quilting lines.

7. Raw edges even, machine baste the cording in place around the outside edges of the bib-collar (Fig. 6-33).

8. Pin and machine baste the ties in place on the sides and center back of the collar (Fig. 6-34). You will need four ties of $\frac{1}{4}''$ ribbon 8″ long for the collar back and four ties of $\frac{3}{4}''$ ribbon 20″ long for the collar sides.

9. Right sides to right sides, pin the collar in place on the lining. Using the basting line for the cording as a guide, machine stitch around the outer edges of the collar, leaving an opening for turning (Fig. 6-35). Trim seams, clip curves, and turn the collar through the opening.

10. Slipstitch the opening closed. Press the collar edges lightly. Slip over the dress and tie in place (Fig. 6-36).

Fig. 6-33

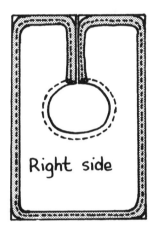

Fig. 6-34

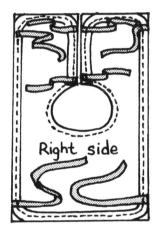

Fig. 6-35

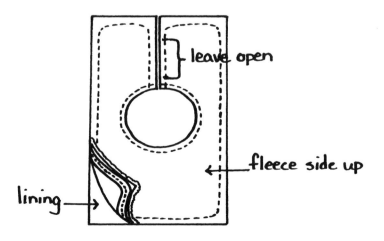

Fig. 6-36

Back View

Rapunzel Pinafore

Rapunzel sits locked away in a hidden tower, but your little princess is sure to stand out in this shadow-appliquéd pinafore (see color section for photograph). Trimmed with satin cording and lace for an elegant effect, it makes a feminine coverup for the simpler garment beneath. Use the same fabric for the pinafore sky and the dress it covers for a coordinated look.

REQUIREMENTS

Yardage (44″ fabric):

Lightweight white fabric (shirting, lawn):

Pinafore skirt, straps, and bib lining:

Size 4—1 yd., size 6—$1\frac{1}{4}$ yds., size 8—$1\frac{1}{2}$ yds., size 10—$1\frac{1}{2}$ yds., size 12—$1\frac{5}{8}$ yds.

Small print on white background—$\frac{1}{4}$ yd. (Bib background. Buy extra for the coordinating dress.)

White voile or batiste—$\frac{1}{4}$ yd.

Fleece—12″ square

Lightweight fusible interfacing—$\frac{1}{4}$ yd.

Assorted fabric scraps (trees, castle, hair, and face)

Satin cording—1 yd.

Ruffled lace—$2\frac{1}{2}$ yds.

Satin ribbon—$1\frac{1}{2}$ yds.

Six-strand embroidery floss for eyes and mouth

Quilting thread

Matching colored thread for machine appliqué and sewing

Three white buttons

DIRECTIONS

1. For the pinafore skirt, cut a 45″ wide piece as long as the skirt length plus 3″. (If you are using very sheer fabric or want extra fullness, you may increase the skirt width up to an additional 45″.)

2. Cut two strap pieces $2\frac{1}{2}$″ wide and long enough to be sewn into the bib front, to criss-cross the child's back, and to button into the skirt band. Cut the waistband 4″ wide and as long as the child's waist plus 2″.

3. If desired, apply fusible interfacing to the pinafore waistband and straps for additional stability and crispness. Cut interfacing only as wide as the finished width of straps and waistband—1″ for the straps and $1\frac{1}{2}$″ for the waistband (Fig. 6-37).

Fig. 6-37

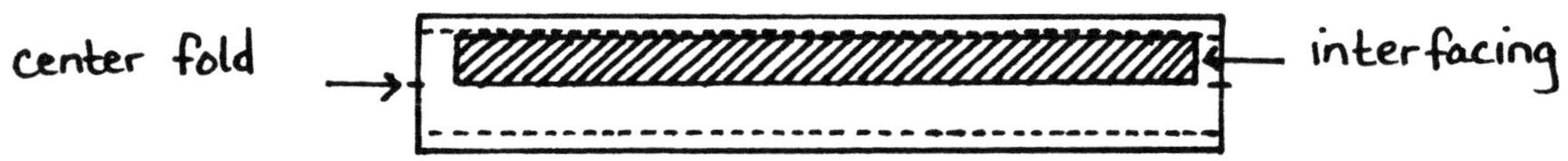

center fold → interfacing

4. Using the oval-shaped pattern given in this chapter, cut the pinafore bib from the background fabric, fleece, sheer overlay, and lining.

5. Cut out shadow appliqués from the fused fabric (Fig. 6-38). Mark the quilting lines on the appliqués with a pencil. Make sure they are dark enough to be seen through the sheer fabric. The quilting lines can also be drawn on the sheer overlay with a water-soluble marker.

6. Using a glue stick or spray adhesive, position the appliqués on the background fabric in the order shown in Figure 6-38 (Fig. 6-39).

7. Embroider details on Rapunzel's face.

8. Pin batting, foundation, and sheer overlay together securely. Baste around the outside edges through all layers. Using deep-colored sewing or quilting thread, quilt through all layers around each appliqué and on the suggested quilting lines.

9. Machine baste the cording in place around the edges of the bib (Fig. 6-40). The raw edges of the cording should match the raw edges of the bib.

10. Machine baste the gathered lace around bib edges just outside the corded edge with the ruffle facing inward (Fig. 6-41).

Fig. 6-38
The design consists of five parts.

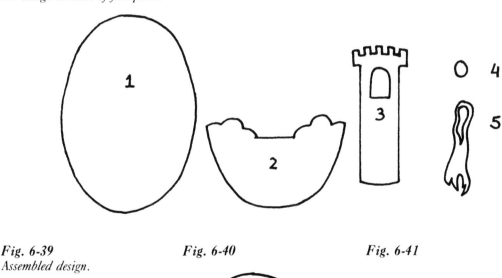

Fig. 6-39
Assembled design.

Fig. 6-40

Fig. 6-41

11. Fold each strap together lengthwise, right sides to right sides, and machine stitch $\frac{1}{4}''$ from the raw edge, leaving one end open for turning (Fig. 6-42). Trim the corner and turn and press.

12. Machine baste the straps in place on the top of the bib. Fold up and pin the straps to prevent them from being caught in stitching when the lining is attached (Fig. 6-43).

13. With right sides together, pin the bib front to the lining and machine stitch with a $\frac{1}{2}''$ seam allowance. Use the basting line for the satin cording as a stitching guide. Leave an opening for turning the oval between the straps (Fig. 6-44). Trim the seam, clip curves, turn, and lightly press seam. Slipstitch the opening closed.

14. Machine hem the pinafore skirt. Sew the lace on the skirt so that the ruffled edge extends just beyond the skirt hem. Sew satin ribbon over the bound edge of the lace (Fig. 6-45).

15. Hem the skirt sides by turning the edges under 1″ twice so that no raw edges show (Fig. 6-46).

16. Using two rows of gathering stitches, gather the top edge of the skirt to fit the waistband. Right sides together, fold the waistband in half lenthwise and stitch ends (Fig. 6-47). Trim the seam, turn, and press. Turn the raw edges to the inside of the waistband and slipstitch closed, concealing the waistband seam (Fig. 6-48).

Fig. 6-42

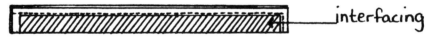

interfacing

Fig. 6-43   *Fig. 6-44*

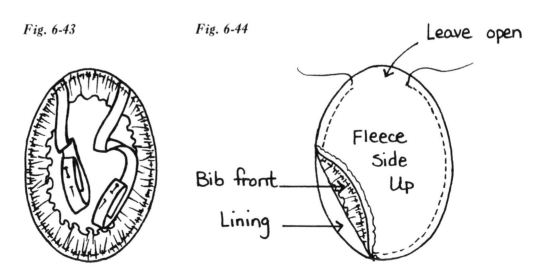

Leave open

Bib front

Lining

Fleece Side Up

17. Center the bib on the pinafore skirt and hand stitch the bib back to the waistband (Fig. 6-49). Stitch the bib front to the waistband, taking small stitches on both sides under the lace edge.
18. Try the pinafore on the child and mark the straps and waistband for buttons and buttonholes. Make buttonholes for the straps and waist closing. Sew the buttons on the straps and the pinafore is ready to wear (Fig. 6-50).

Fig. 6-45

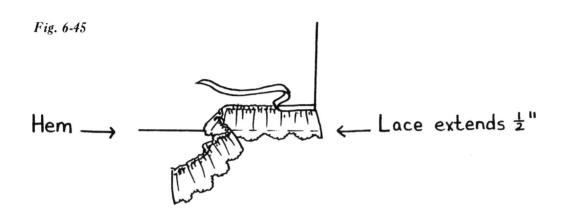

Hem → ← Lace extends ½"

Fig. 6-46   *Fig. 6-47*   *Fig. 6-48*

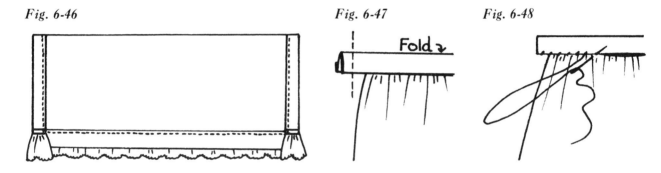

Fold

Fig. 6-49   *Fig. 6-50*

wrong side

Fairy Princess Pillows

Any or all of these pillows (see color section for photograph) would make a charming addition to the "Once Upon a Time" quilt. Each uses shadow appliqué and is similar to a garment already shown in this chapter. When necessary, refer to the garment instructions for more information.

REQUIREMENTS

Heart-Shaped Sleeping Beauty Pillow (12" × 14")

Yardage:

> White broadcloth—$\frac{1}{2}$ yd. (background fabric and pillow back)
> White voile or batiste—$\frac{3}{4}$ yd. (sheer overlay and ruffle)
> Lightweight fusible interfacing—$\frac{1}{4}$ yd.
> Assorted fabric scraps (carriage, door, wheels, stem, and slippers)

Pink satin cording—1 yd.

Ruffled lace—1 yd.

Quilting thread

Matching colored thread for appliqué and sewing

Round Cinderella Pillow (10" diameter)

Yardage:

> White broadcloth—$\frac{1}{2}$ yd. (pillow back and ruffle)
> White voile or batiste—$\frac{1}{3}$ yd. (sheer overlay)
> Fleece—12" square
> Turquoise/blue solid—$\frac{1}{3}$ yd. (background fabric)
> Lightweight fusible interfacing—$\frac{1}{4}$ yd.
> Assorted fabric scraps (carriage, door, wheels, stem, and slippers)

Pink satin cording—1 yd.

Ruffled lace—1 yd.

Quilting thread

Matching colored thread for appliqué and sewing

Oval Rapunzel Pillow (7" × 9")

Yardage:

> Light print—$\frac{1}{2}$ yd. (foundation, pillow back, and ruffle)
> White voile or batiste—$\frac{1}{4}$ yd. (sheer overlay)
> Fleece—12" square
> Lightweight fusible interfacing—$\frac{1}{4}$ yd.
> Assorted fabric scraps (trees, castle, hair, and face)

Satin cording—1 yd.

Ruffled lace—1 yd.

Six-strand embroidery floss for eyes and mouth

Quilting thread

Matching colored thread for appliqué and sewing

DIRECTIONS

1. Refer to the "Shadow Appliqué" section in Chapter 1.
2. Make a paper pattern for the desired pillow shape using the dimensions given in the "Requirements" section. Be sure to add seam allowances. Cut the pillow batting, foundation, and sheer overlay from this pattern.
3. When making pillows, we prefer to make a simple flap closure in the back, like a pillow sham. This allows the inner pillow or form to be removed easily for laundering. To make the pillow back, cut a rectangle 6″ wider than the dimension given. For example, the rectangle for the 10″ round pillow back will measure 11″ × 17″. This includes a $\frac{1}{2}$″ seam allowance plus the 4″ overlap. Cut the rectangle in half, making two smaller rectangles measuring 11″ × 8$\frac{1}{2}$″. Set aside.
4. Follow step 4 of the "Once upon a time" quilt instructions for cutting out and marking the appliqués. The quilting lines can be drawn on the sheer overlay with a water-soluble marker.
5. Using a glue stick or spray adhesive, position the appliqués on background fabric (Fig. 6-51).
6. Embroider details on the appliqués.
7. Refer to Step 6 of the Sleeping Beauty vest instructions for pinning, basting,

Fig. 6-51

A

B

C

and quilting the pillows. If necessary, check the instructions for other companion garments for more detail.

8. Machine baste the cording in place around the edges of the pillow. Cording is applied to pillows in the same way that it is for the Rapunzel pinafore bib front in step 9 (see Fig. 6-40).

9. Machine baste the gathered lace around the pillow edges just outside the corded edge with ruffle facing inward (see Fig. 6-41).

10. Fabric ruffle: Measure the distance around the entire outside edge of the pillow. The ruffle should be at least two times this distance. (You may make it up to three times the distance if you wish.) Cut enough strips of fabric 5″ wide to equal this length. Right sides to right sides, sew them together with $\frac{1}{4}″$ seams to make a large loop (Fig. 6-52).

11. Fold the loop in half lengthwise with the wrong sides together and press.

12. Divide the ruffle into two sections with pins. Make two rows of gathering stitches on the raw edges of the ruffle, breaking the stitching at the pins (Fig. 6-53).

13. Divide the pillow front in half and mark with straight pins. Draw up the gathering threads so that the ruffle matches the pillow front. Pin in place, matching the raw edges of the ruffle and the pillow (Fig. 6-54). Turn the pillow over and machine stitch the ruffle in place using the basting lines for the cording and lace as a guide. Make sure you pivot carefully at the corners of the heart to avoid catching the edges of the lace and ruffle in the stitching.

Fig. 6-52

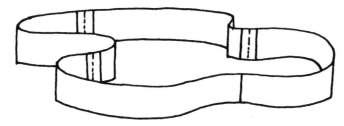

Fig. 6-54

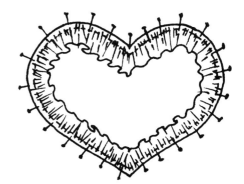

Fig. 6-53

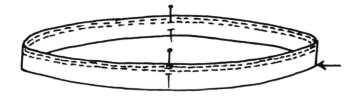

14. For the pillow back, take the two previously cut rectangles and press under 1″ on one of the lengthwise edges. Fold and press under 1″ again. Machine stitch in place (Fig. 6-55).

15. Lapping hemmed edge, lay the rectangles on top of each other wrong side to right side. Baste together across the hemmed edge (Fig. 6-56).

16. Right sides together, center the pillow front on the pillow back and pin in place (Fig. 6-57). Using the basting stitches for the cording and lace as a guide, stitch the pillow front and back together. Trim seams, clip curves, and turn.

17. Stuff the pillow with a home- or ready-made pillow form. A snap or Velcro may be added to the flap closure if desired.

Fig. 6-55   *Fig. 6-56* 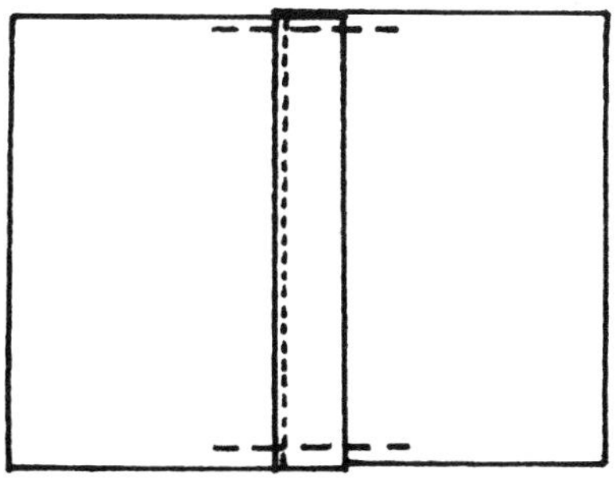   *Fig. 6-57*

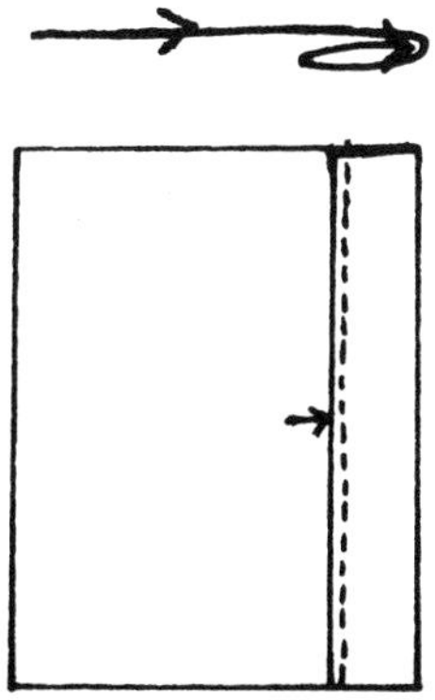

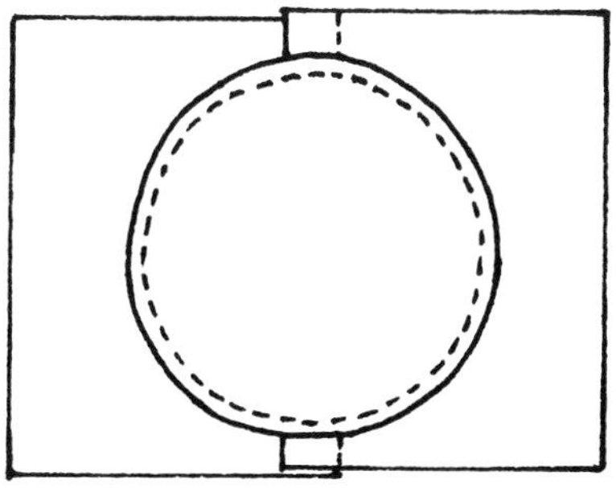

PATTERNS▶

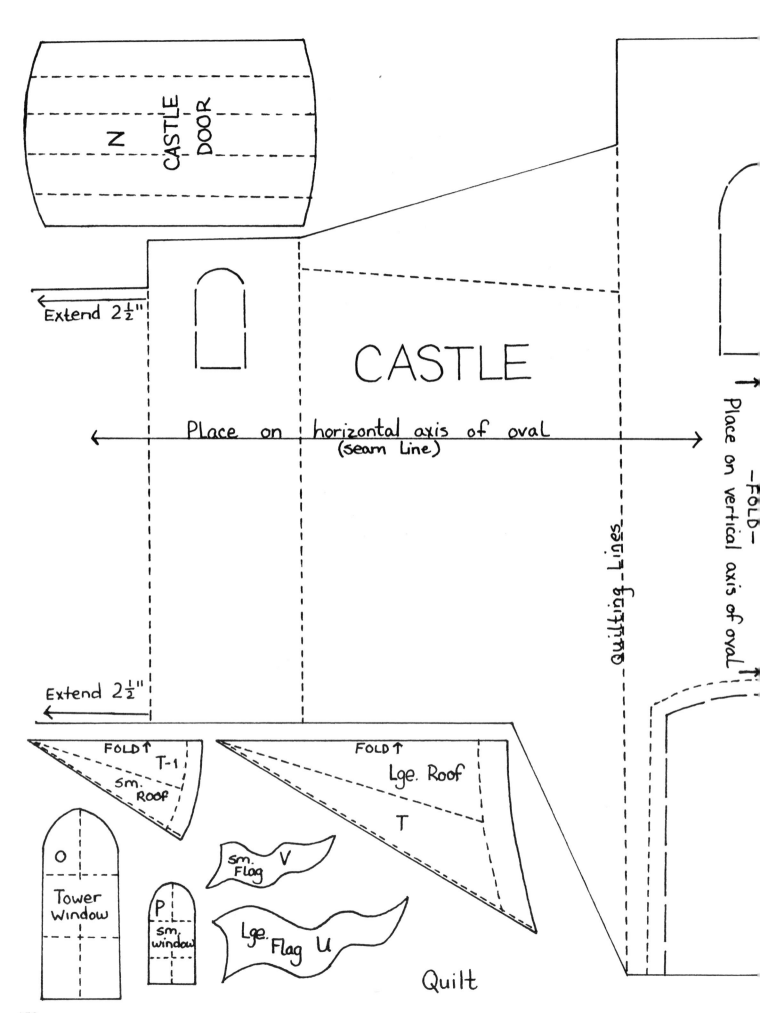

N

CASTLE DOOR

Extend 2½"

CASTLE

Place on horizontal axis of oval
(seam line)

Extend 2½"

—FOLD—
Place on vertical axis of oval

Quilting lines

FOLD↑   T-1
sm.
ROOF

FOLD↑   Lge. Roof

T

O
Tower
Window

P
sm.
window

sm.
Flag   V

Lge. Flag   U

Quilt

158

G SCROLL
Cut 1 reverse
Grain

G-1 SCROLL
CUT 1
Grain

E SCROLL

Once upon

Grain

↓ Tape Broken Lines Together ↓

F SCROLL

CUT 1
CUT 1 reverse

Grain

A

Quilt

159

↑ Tape Broken Lines Together ↑

a time...

M

L-9

S

L-8

L-7

R

Q

Quilt

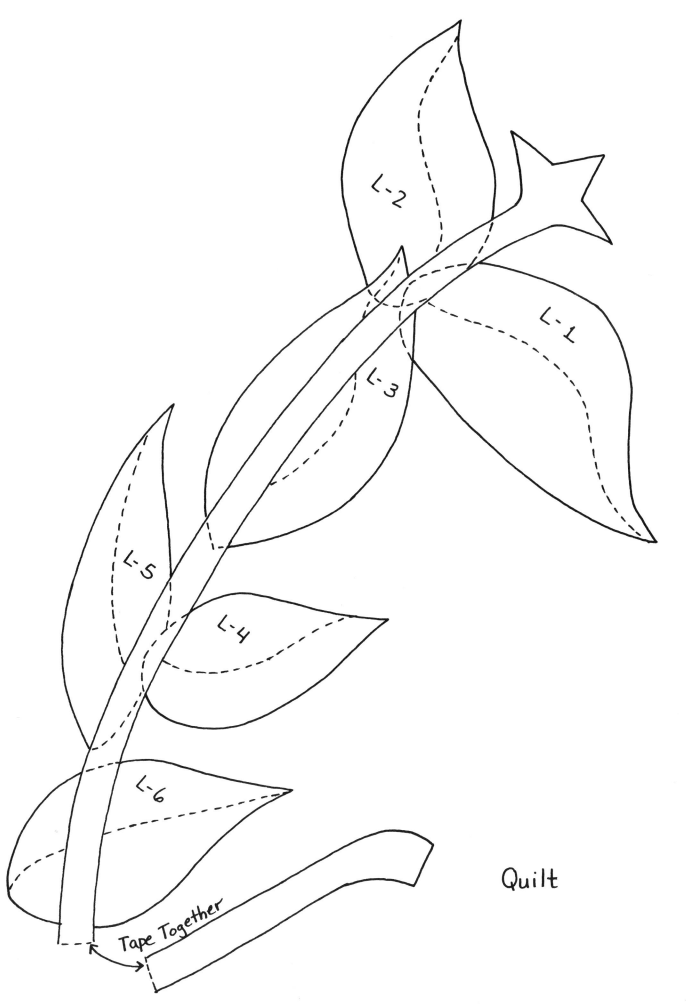

L-2

L-1

L-3

L-5

L-4

L-6

Quilt

Tape Together

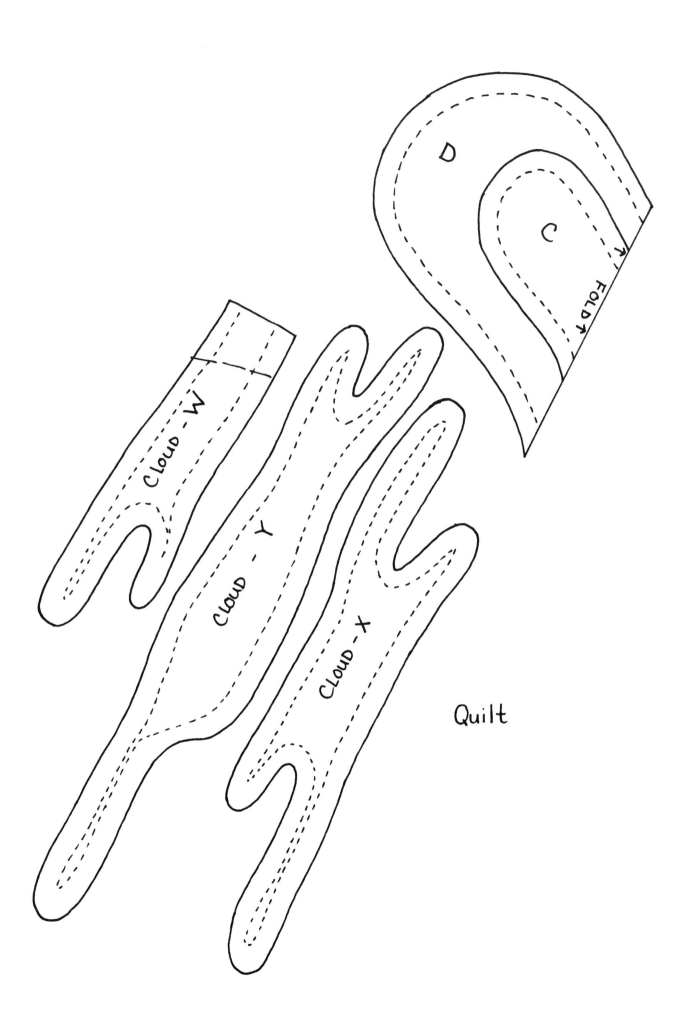

Cloud - W

Cloud - Y

Cloud - X

D

C

FOLD

Quilt

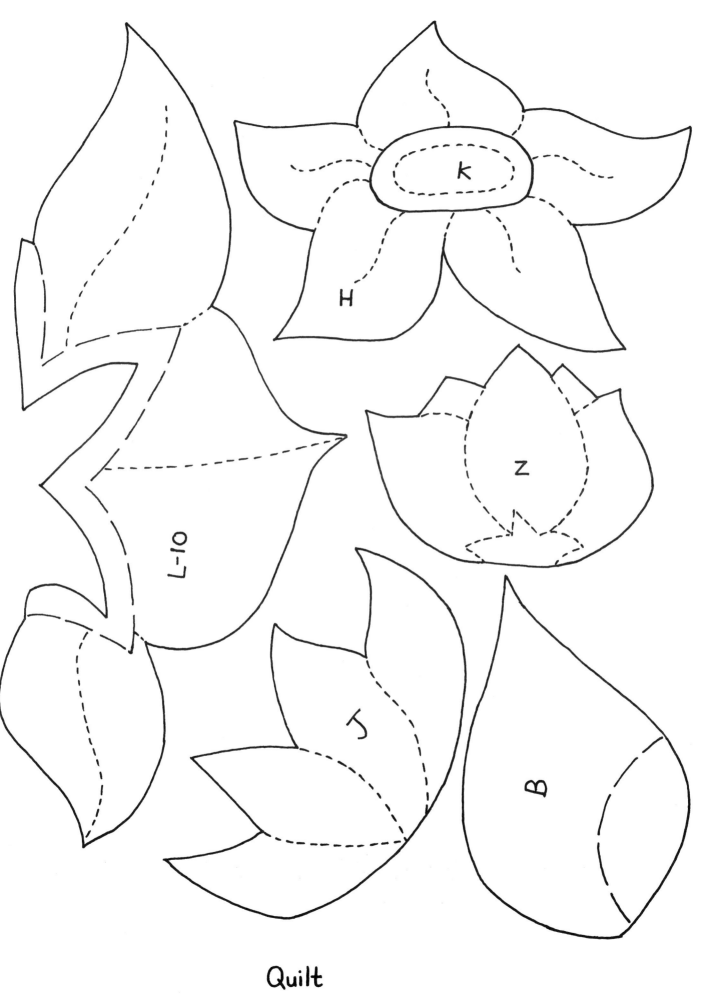

Quilt

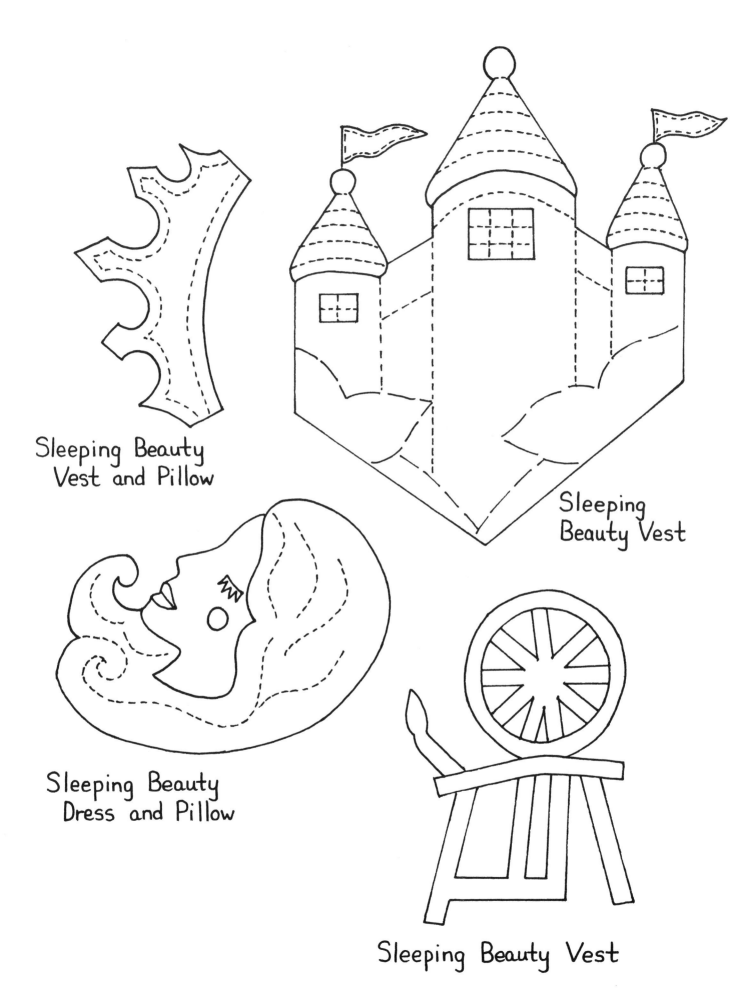

Sleeping Beauty
Vest and Pillow

Sleeping
Beauty Vest

Sleeping Beauty
Dress and Pillow

Sleeping Beauty Vest

164

Sleeping
Beauty
Dress

Assorted Tendrils –

Sleeping
Beauty
Vest
Dress
Pillow

Sleeping Beauty
Vest and Pillow

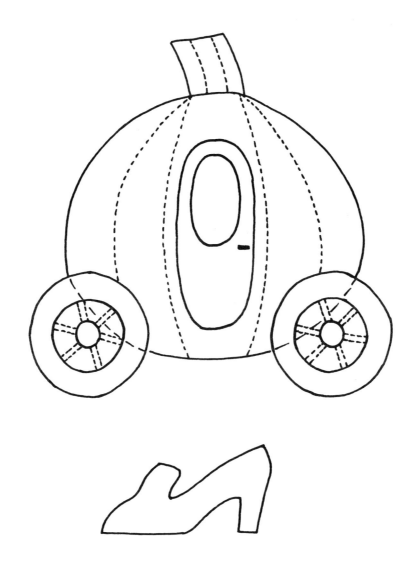

Cinderella Bib-Collar and Pillow

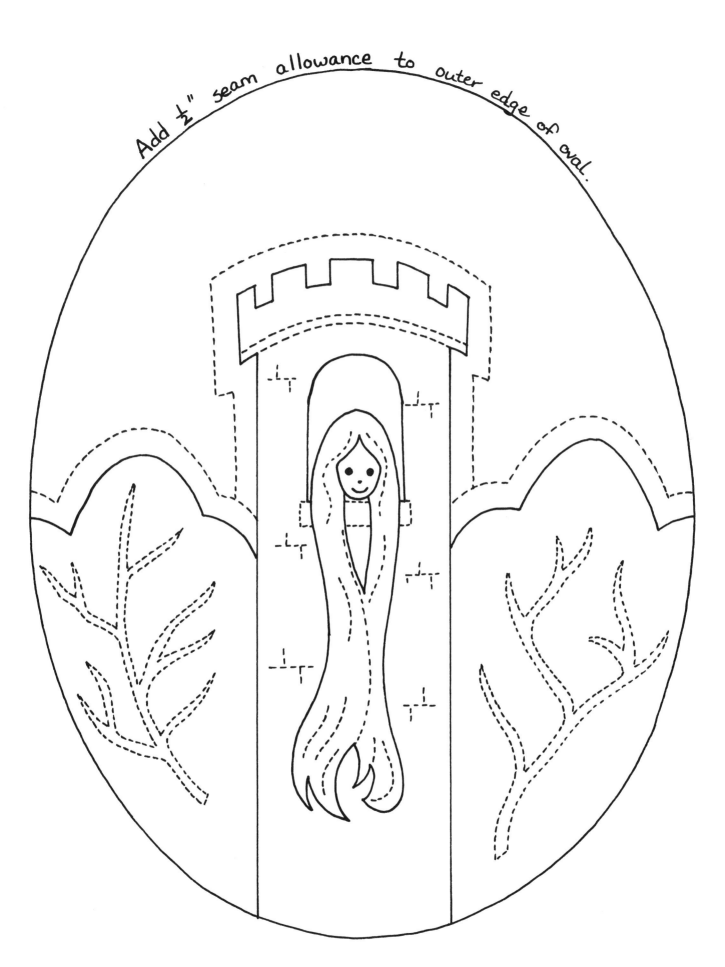

Add ½" seam allowance to outer edge of oval.

Rapunzel Pinafore and Pillow

Chapter 7

Jack and the Beanstalk

Fig. 7-1
"Fe, Fi, Fo, Fum" quilt.

Fig. 7-2
Jack and the Beanstalk vest (front).

Fig. 7-3
Jack and the Beanstalk vest (back).

170

Fig. 7-4
Beanstalk growth chart.

Fig. 7-5
Drawstring "Bag of Gold" and "BEANS" trinket bag.

171

Jack's adventures upon climbing the beanstalk provide the background for the quilt, vest, growth chart, and other items presented in this chapter.

"Fe, Fi, Fo, Fum" Quilt

The "Fe, Fi, Fo, Fum" quilt (see color selection for photograph) features large figures and letters that can be machine appliquéd for speed and durability. When choosing the fabrics for this quilt top, select the inside border fabric (stripe) first, and then coordinate the other fabrics with it. The finished quilt is 59″ × 95″ (twin-bed size).

REQUIREMENTS

Yardage (44″ fabric):

> Light blue-green—$2\frac{1}{4}$ yds. ($39\frac{1}{2}$″ × $75\frac{1}{2}$″ rectangle)
>
> Dark-green and red stripe—1 yd. if stripe is printed on diagonal; $1\frac{1}{2}$ yds. if stripe is printed vertically (beanstalk and two each of leaf patterns A and B, plus one reverse of pattern A and two reverse of pattern B)
>
> Dark red—$\frac{1}{2}$ yd. (letters)
>
> Dark-green solid—$\frac{1}{3}$ yd. (two each of leaf pattern A, A reverse, and B, plus one reverse of pattern B)
>
> Striped fabric (inside border)—yardage depends on the repeat of the stripe along the width of the fabric. The striped fabric shown in Figure 7-1 required $2\frac{1}{4}$ yds. The minimum amount needed for a solid or print fabric where the border is cut on the crosswise of goods is 1 yd. (inside border strips, four of pattern C and four of reverse)
>
> Dark-green print—2 yds. (outside border strips, four of pattern D and four of reverse, continuous bias)
>
> White solid—$\frac{1}{4}$ yd. (cloud)
>
> Quilt lining—6 yds.
>
> Batting—65″ × 100″ rectangle
>
> Fusible interfacing—2 yds.

Quilting thread

Coordinated thread for machine appliqué and sewing

DIRECTIONS

1. Enlarge leaf pattern A and B according to the instructions in Chapter 1. The leaf must be enlarged to twice its size. Using Figure 7-6 as a guide, make patterns for the following letters: *FE* (each letter 3″ × 5″), *FI* (each letter 5″ × 7″), *FO* (each letter 7″ × 9″), and *FUM* (each letter 9″ × 11″)

2. From the striped fabric for the inside border, cut two horizontal strips $4\frac{1}{2}$″ × $39\frac{1}{2}$″ and two vertical strips $4\frac{1}{2}$″ × $75\frac{1}{2}$″. From the dark-green print, cut two strips $6\frac{1}{2}$″ × $39\frac{1}{2}$″ and four strips $6\frac{1}{2}$″ × 38″. Next cut 9 yds. of $1\frac{1}{4}$″-wide continuous bias made from an 18″ square. (See instructions in Chapter 1 on making continuous bias.)

3. Cut out the letters and all other pieces according to the instructions given in "Yardage" section. See next step for instructions on cutting the beanstalk,

Fig. 7-6

Scale : $\frac{1}{10}$ " = 1"

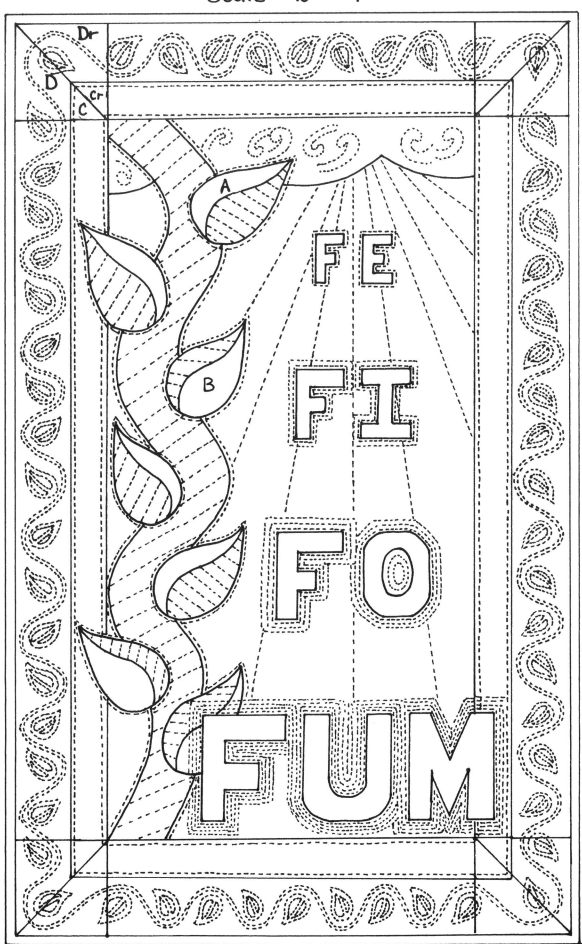

step 11 for corner pieces. Pay special attention to Figures 7-1 and 7-6 and to the cutting instructions for the leaves. Apply fusible interfacing to all appliqué fabrics except the cloud fabric before cutting.

4. The beanstalk is 6″ wide and can be cut on the length or crosswise grain if the stripe is printed on the bias. If the stripe is printed on the lengthwise of fabric, the beanstalk must be positioned and cut on the bias. Refer to Figure 7-6 for scaled drawing. It will be easier to make in two pieces because of its length. Seam it in the middle, approximately 43″ from the top. Sew straight across the grain of the fabric and match the diagonal stripe for a continuous look (Fig. 7-7).

5. Position all pattern pieces on the quilt top and trace around them with a pencil or water-soluble marker to ensure correct placement.

6. Pin, baste, or glue-stick the cloud in place. Using a zigzag stitch, sew the curved edges to the background fabric. Once the cloud edges are held securely, satin stitch the edges to give a smooth finish.

7. Straight stitch the edges of the beanstalk and leaves to the background fabric to prevent slipping and bunching. For leaves that extend into the border, stop stitching within 2″ of the edge (Fig. 7-8). Stitching can be completed once the borders are attached. Satin stitch the leaves and beanstalk. Stitch around the striped leaf sections with contrasting thread.

Fig. 7-7   *Fig. 7-8*

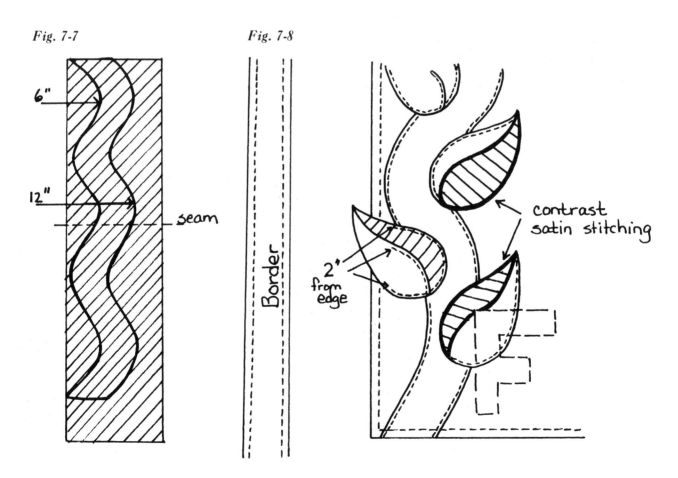

8. Beginning with *FE*, glue-stick the letters on the quilt top. Straight stitch around the edges, then satin stitch in place. Be sure to recheck the position of the letters to make certain they are straight on the background. Part of the letter *M* will have to be sewn down after the striped border is attached.

9. Attach the striped borders to the long sides with $\frac{1}{4}''$ seam allowances and finish appliquéing the leaves and the letter *M* (Fig. 7-9).

10. Right sides together, sew the short sides of the $6\frac{1}{2}'' \times 38''$ strips together with $\frac{1}{4}''$ seam allowances to make two outer border strips, each measuring $6\frac{1}{2}'' \times 75\frac{1}{2}''$. Attach these long borders to the striped borders on both sides of the quilt (Fig. 7-10). Press the quilt top keeping all seams out.

11. Referring to Figures 7-6 and 7-11, make pattern pieces for mitered corners. Begin by making a 10″ square from poster board or cardboard. Divide the square in half diagonally from the upper left-hand corner to the lower right-hand corner. Make a box 4″ square in the lower right-hand corner (Fig. 7-11). Cut the square apart on marked lines for mitered-corner pattern pieces C, Cr, D, and Dr. From the striped fabric, cut four of pattern C and four of reverse pattern C. From the dark-green print, cut four of pattern D and four of reverse pattern D. Be sure to add $\frac{1}{4}''$ seam allowances *before* cutting. Matching the corners will be easier if you place the triangle pattern on the border print carefully (Fig. 7-12).

Fig. 7-9

Fig. 7-10

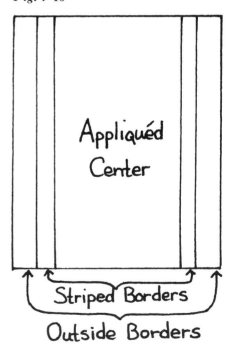

12. Sew the C and D corner sections together with the reverse pieces to form large triangles (Fig. 7-13A). Then sew the triangles together to complete the corner block (Fig. 7-13B).

13. Sew each remaining $4\frac{1}{2}'' \times 39\frac{1}{2}''$ border strip to the $6\frac{1}{2}'' \times 39\frac{1}{2}''$ strips to make two border strips measuring $10\frac{1}{2}'' \times 39\frac{1}{2}''$ each.

14. Attach the corners to the short border strips (Fig. 7-14) and press.

15. Right sides together, matching seams, attach the shorter border strips to the quilt and press.

16. Trim the light blue-green quilt background from behind the appliqués to reduce bulk and make quilting easier.

17. Referring to Figure 7-6, mark quilt top with a pencil or water-soluble marker. A white or silver architect's pencil works well for marking dark fabrics. Use leaf and vine patterns in the pattern section to mark the vine on the border.

Fig. 7-11

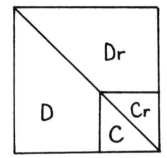

Fig. 7-12

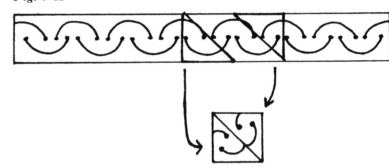

Fig. 7-13

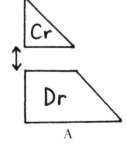

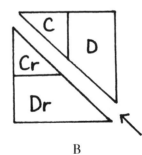

A   B

Fig. 7-14

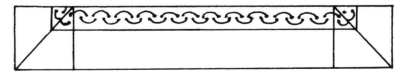

18. Baste the quilt top together with the batting and lining.
19. Quilt in the seam line around the appliqués. Then quilt along borders and on the suggested quilting lines. For the descending letters, quilt in the seam line around each letter and $\frac{1}{4}''$ out. On the letters *FI*, quilt again $\frac{1}{2}''$ away from the $\frac{1}{4}''$ line. Continue adding quilting lines at $\frac{1}{2}''$ increments as letters increase in size to the bottom of the quilt (see Fig. 7-6).
20. Trim away the excess batting and lining fabric. Bind the quilt with the self-made continuous bias.

Jack and the Beanstalk Vest

On the front of this hand-appliquéd and hand-quilted vest, Jack, fleeing the giant, runs home. On the back, the giant's boot descends the beanstalk (see color section for photograph). The detail on these figures lends itself better to hand, rather than machine, appliqué.

REQUIREMENTS

Commercial pattern in child's size—one back and one front piece; no darts, princess lines, or lapels.

Yardage (44″ fabric):

Dark-green solid—$\frac{1}{2}$ to $\frac{3}{4}$ yd., depending on pattern requirements (vest back and front)

Dark-green print—$\frac{1}{2}$ to $\frac{3}{4}$ yd. (vest lining)

White solid—$\frac{1}{4}$ yd. (cloud)

Light-green stripe—$\frac{1}{4}$ yd. (leaves and continuous bias $1\frac{1}{4}'' \times 30''$)

Fleece—same as for dark-green solid

Assorted 100-percent cotton fabric scraps (Jack, house, boot)

Black, yellow, and red embroidery floss

Quilting thread

Coordinated thread for appliqué and sewing

Three buttons—choose ones that look like beans

DIRECTIONS

1. Note the method of adapting a commercial vest pattern in Chapter 1. Cut out the vest, lining, and fleece according to the pattern instructions.
2. Position a large sheet of paper over the vest back to make the pattern for the cloud insert (Fig. 7-15). Trim to fit the shoulder and armholes evenly. Using this pattern, cut the cloud insert from the white fabric.
3. Make 30″ (this may vary according to child's size) of continuous bias from the green-striped fabric to use for the beanstalk. (See instructions in Chapter 1 and refer to Figures 7-3 and 7-16 for the general shape of the beanstalk.) Cut 14 leaves from the remaining fabric. Position the beanstalk over the insert on vest and slipstitch in place (Fig. 7-16). Trim the dark fabric from behind the cloud insert, leaving a $\frac{1}{4}''$ seam allowance on the edges to prevent it from casting a shadow through the white fabric.

4. Position the leaves (Figs. 7-16 and 7-17) with pins or glue stick, and appliqué them in place.

5. Using the appliqué patterns, trace Jack, the boot, and the house on the background fabric (Fig. 7-17). Pin or glue-stick the appliqués in place and begin slipstitching, matching the pencil line on the appliqué to the pencil outline on the background fabric. Appliqué the pieces in the following order: Jack (legs, hand, face, hair, shirt, hen, and sleeve); the giant's boot (leg, heel, sole, shoe, and buckle); house (path, house, window, door, roof, and chimney).

6. Embroider details on the giant's shoe with three strands of black embroidery floss (see the boot pattern). Also use black floss to make French knots for

Fig. 7-15

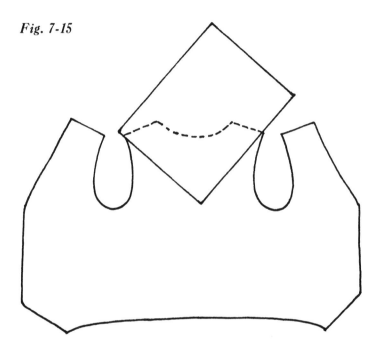

Fig. 7-16

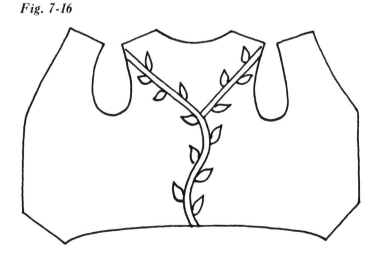

eyes for Jack and the hen. Complete the hen by embroidering the comb, wattle, and beak using a satin stitch with two strands of red and yellow floss.

7. Leaving shoulder seams open, sew the vest, lining, and batting together, layering vest and lining right sides together with fleece on top (Fig. 7-18).

8. Trim seams, clip curves, and turn the vest through the shoulder openings.

9. Mark the quilting lines on the vest with a pencil, using a ruler and the back yoke as a guide (Fig. 7-19).

10. Join the shoulder seams by hand using small stitches and sewing securely. Trim the batting out of the seam allowances. Slipstitch lining closed.

11. Quilt the vest with matching thread. Any heavy thread or buttonhole twist coated with beeswax will work if matching quilting thread cannot be found.

12. Make buttonholes and sew on buttons to finish.

Fig. 7-17

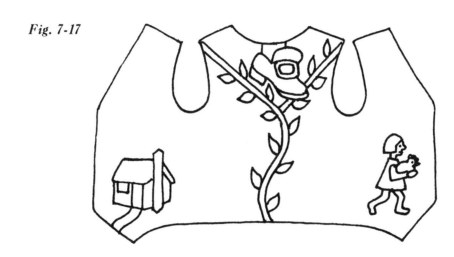

Fig. 7-18

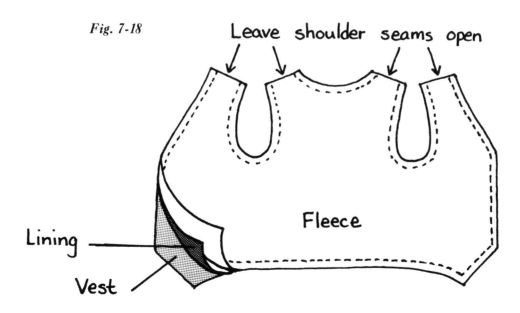

Fig. 7-19
Suggested quilting lines. Quilt in the seam line around the leaves,
vine, shoe, house, and Jack. Quilt again $\frac{1}{4}''$ around the house and
Jack.

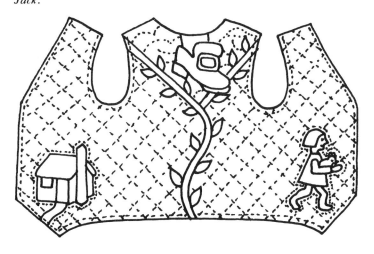

Beanstalk Growth Chart

Check and record your child's growth on the beanstalk growth chart (see color section for photograph). Like the vest details, the details on the growth chart lend themselves more to hand, rather than machine, appliqué. The finished growth chart measures 13″ × 42″.

REQUIREMENTS

Yardage (44″ fabric):

> Dark green—$\frac{1}{2}$ yd. ($13\frac{1}{2}''$ × $42\frac{1}{2}''$ rectangle)
>
> Green print—$\frac{3}{4}$ yd. (14″ × 44″ rectangle for lining, 14 leaves, and bias for beanstalk)
>
> White solid—scrap (clouds)
>
> Assorted 100-percent cotton fabric scraps—(Jack, boot)
>
> Bias or striped fabric to finish growth chart—$3\frac{1}{2}$ yds. × $1\frac{1}{2}''$ (*Note:* If you use a vertical stripe from your own fabric rather than commercial bias, yardages may vary according to the regularity of the stripe. You will probably need at least $1\frac{1}{4}$ yds. to avoid piecing on the lengthwise side.)
>
> Batting—$\frac{1}{2}$ yd. (14″ × 44″ rectangle)

Red, yellow, and black embroidery floss

Green quilting thread

Coordinated thread for machine appliqué and sewing

Curtain rings—optional (for hanging)

DIRECTIONS

1. Cut out the lining, batting, and background fabric according to the dimensions given in the "Yardage" section. Cut out remaining appliqués, except the beanstalk and cloud, remembering to add a scant $\frac{1}{4}''$ seam allowance for hand

Fig. 7-20

181
*Jack and
the Beanstalk*

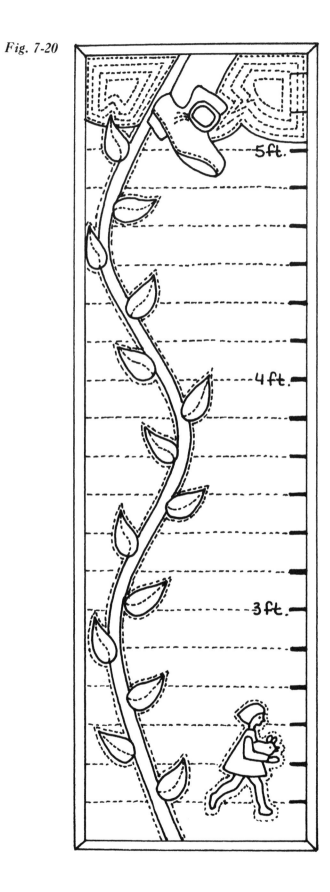

appliqué. Be sure to leave at least a 9″ square of the green-print fabric intact to make the bias for the beanstalk.

2. Referring to Figure 7-20, make a paper pattern for the cloud. (Slight variations in cloud size are acceptable.) Using the pattern, cut the cloud from the white fabric, making sure to add seam allowances for hand appliqué. Pin the cloud to the background and stitch in place. Trim the dark background from behind the cloud, leaving a $\frac{1}{4}$″ seam allowance on the edges to prevent it from casting a shadow through the white fabric.

3. Make 45″ of $1\frac{1}{4}$″-wide continuous bias from the green-print fabric to use for the beanstalk. (See the instructions in Chapter 1 and refer to Figures 7-4 and 7-20 for general shape of the beanstalk.) Position the beanstalk on the background fabric and slipstitch in place using the method described for hand appliquéing the bias in Chapter 1 (see Fig. 7-20). The beanstalk should be $\frac{3}{4}$″ wide after it is sewn down.

4. Position the leaves with pins or glue stick, and appliqué them in place (see Fig. 7-20).

5. Follow step 5 of the vest instructions, omitting the house appliqué. Refer to Figure 7-20 for placement.

6. Follow step 6 of the vest instructions.

7. Mark horizontal lines $1\frac{1}{2}$″ long at 2″ intervals along the right side of the growth chart. Embroider with red floss the labels "3 ft.", "4 ft.", and "5 ft." at one-foot intervals (see Fig. 7-20). (The chart will hang two feet from the floor.) Embroider the horizontal lines with red floss.

8. Mark the quilting lines with a light-colored pencil or water-soluble marker (see Fig. 7-20). Baste the lining and batting to the growth chart and quilt on the suggested quilting lines. When quilting is complete, trim the edges of the lining and batting even with the front.

9. Bind the growth chart with commercial bias, self-made bias, or striped fabric strips, mitering the corners according to the instructions in Chapter 1. (It is not necessary to use bias for binding, so don't be afraid to use a vertical stripe from the lengthwise of fabric to achieve an interesting effect. Remember to cut strips at least $1\frac{1}{2}$″ wide.)

10. Add fabric loops, thread loops, or curtain rings to the back for ease in hanging.

Drawstring "Bag of Gold"

The drawstring "Bag of Gold" (see color section for photograph) is quick and easy to make. Letters and coins are machine appliquéd. The bag can be used as a pillow or pajama bag to complement the "Fe, Fi, Fo, Fum" quilt, or it may be used alone to tote or store secret treasures. The finished bag measures 13″ × $16\frac{1}{2}$″.

REQUIREMENTS

Yardage (44″ fabric):

Tan twill or denim (medium weight)—$\frac{1}{2}$ yd. ($17\frac{1}{2}$″ × 27″ rectangle)

Gold print—$\frac{1}{2}$ yd. ($17\frac{1}{2}$″ × 27″ rectangle for lining; four coins)

Green solid—$\frac{1}{4}$ yd. (letters)

Gold bias, commercial or self-made—1 yd. (seam casing)

Green-solid or green-print bias, commercial or self-made—2 yds. (drawstrings)

Fusible interfacing—$\frac{1}{4}$ yd.

Coordinated thread for machine appliqué and sewing

DIRECTIONS

1. Cut the bag and lining. Cut the letters and coins from fabric that has been fused to interfacing, and position them with pins or glue stick (Fig. 7-21). Machine appliqué them in place with matching thread.

2. Right sides together, sew the appliquéd bag into a cylinder lengthwise with a $\frac{1}{2}''$ seam allowance (Fig. 7-22). Repeat with the lining. Press the seam open.

3. Wrong sides out, with the bottom opening of the bag matched to the opening end of the lining cylinder, stitch together with a $\frac{1}{2}''$ seam allowance (Fig. 7-23). Trim the seam and clip the corners.

4. Turn the bag so that the seams are enclosed and the only raw edges showing are at the top of the bag (Fig. 7-24). Pin or baste together the raw edges and turn them under $\frac{1}{4}''$. Turn them under again $\frac{1}{4}''$ toward the gold lining to make a clean finished edge (Fig. 7-25).

5. Leaving $1\frac{1}{4}''$ space at the top of the bag, make $\frac{3}{4}''$ vertical buttonholes directly opposite each other on the sides of the bag (Fig. 7-26).

6. Turn the bag lining-side-out and machine stitch a gold bias strip $\frac{3}{4}''$ wide to the front and back of the bag to form a casing. Be sure to turn under the short ends of the bias so that no raw edges show (Fig. 7-27).

7. To make the ties, cut the green bias into two strips, each 1 yard long. Fold them in half with the folded edges together and machine stitch them together lengthwise (Fig. 7-28).

Fig. 7-21

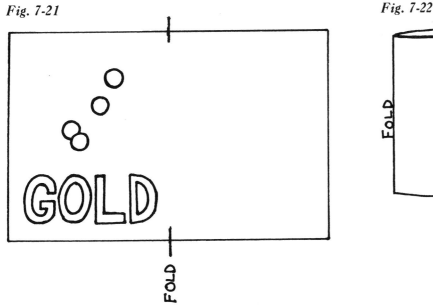

Fig. 7-22

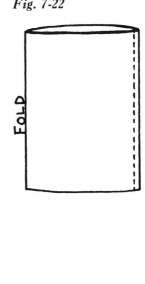

Fig. 7-23

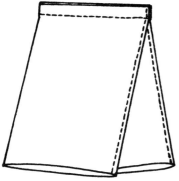

Fig. 7-24

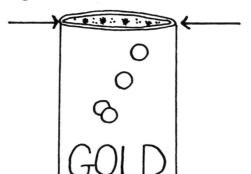

Fig. 7-25

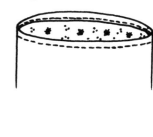

Fig. 7-26

Fig. 7-27

Fig. 7-28

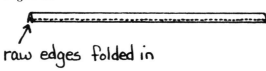

raw edges folded in

Fig. 7-29

8. Using a safety pin, thread one tie through the front and back casings and bring it out again through the same buttonhole it entered. Repeat the process with the other tie, beginning on opposite side (Fig. 7-29). Knot the ends together to prevent them from pulling out. Pulling both ties at the same time should gather the bag evenly at the top.

"BEANS" Marble or Trinket Bag

The "BEANS" bag (see color section for photograph) could be used to carry magic seeds, but most children will find it more useful for marbles, pennies, or other everyday items. Simple and quick to construct, it might be just the thing as a bazaar item. The finished bag measures 5″ × 7″.

REQUIREMENTS

Yardage (44″ fabric):
    Green print—6″ × 15″ rectangle
    Solid-green scrap fused to interfacing—1½″ × 3″ rectangle (letters)
Six-strand red embroidery floss or perle cotton
Red and green thread for sewing and machine appliqué

DIRECTIONS

1. Cut out pieces for the bag and the "BEANS" label and fuse them.
2. Transfer the markings for the "BEANS" label onto a 1½″ × 3″ rectangle with a white pencil or marker that can be easily seen.
3. Machine appliqué the label to the green-print rectangle 5″ down from one of the narrow sides (Fig. 7-30). Satin stitch over the letters, just as you would for machine appliqué, to make the label. Start and stop each letter by machine sewing up and down in the same spot to make a pigtail knot, which will prevent the stitching from pulling out.

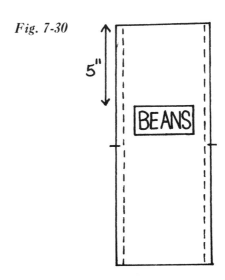

Fig. 7-30

4. Right sides together, fold the rectangle in half crosswise and stitch the sides, taking a ½″ seam allowance (Fig. 7-31). Trim seams, clip corners, turn, and press.

5. Hem the top of the bag by turning under the raw edge ¼″ twice and stitching (Fig. 7-32).

6. Thread an embroidery needle with an 18″ length of perle cotton or six-strand embroidery floss. Leaving at least 3″ of thread hanging, thread the floss in and out of the top of the bag with a running stitch ½″ from the finished edge. Sew all the way around the bag, finishing where you began. Leave another 3″ thread hanging (Fig. 7-33). Knot the ends together and trim them. Repeat with another 18″ length of floss, beginning on the opposite side (Fig. 7-34).

7. The bag should gather evenly when both strings are pulled.

Fig. 7-31

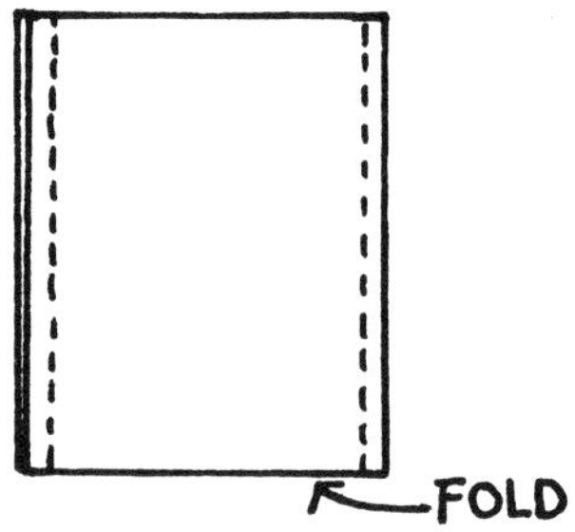

Fig. 7-32

Fig. 7-33

Fig. 7-34

PATTERNS▶

Scaled Template − $\frac{1}{2}'' = 1''$

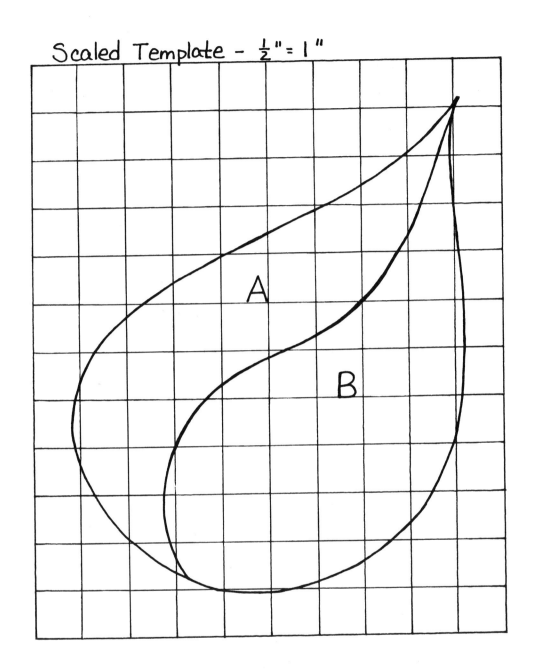

A

B

Quilt

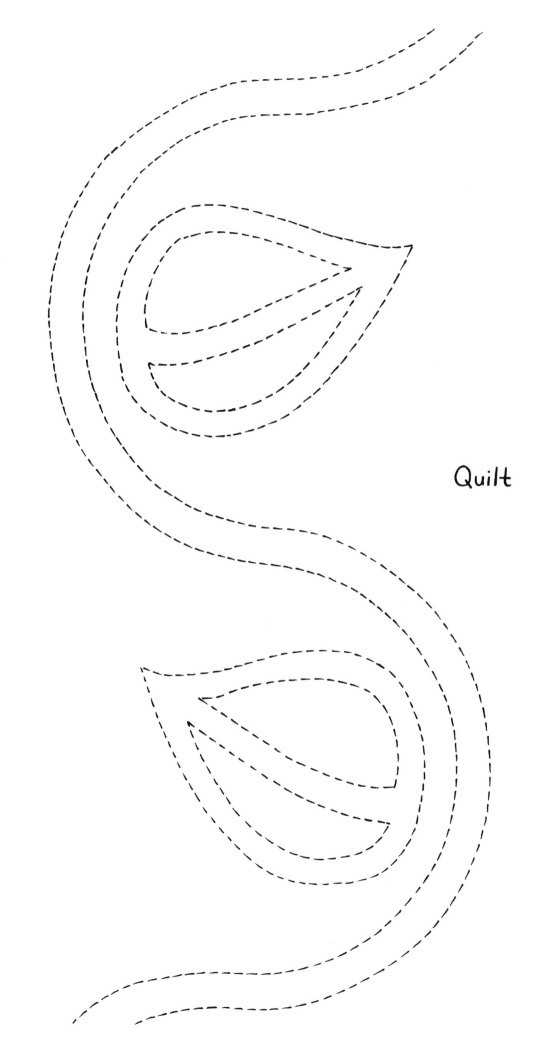

Quilt

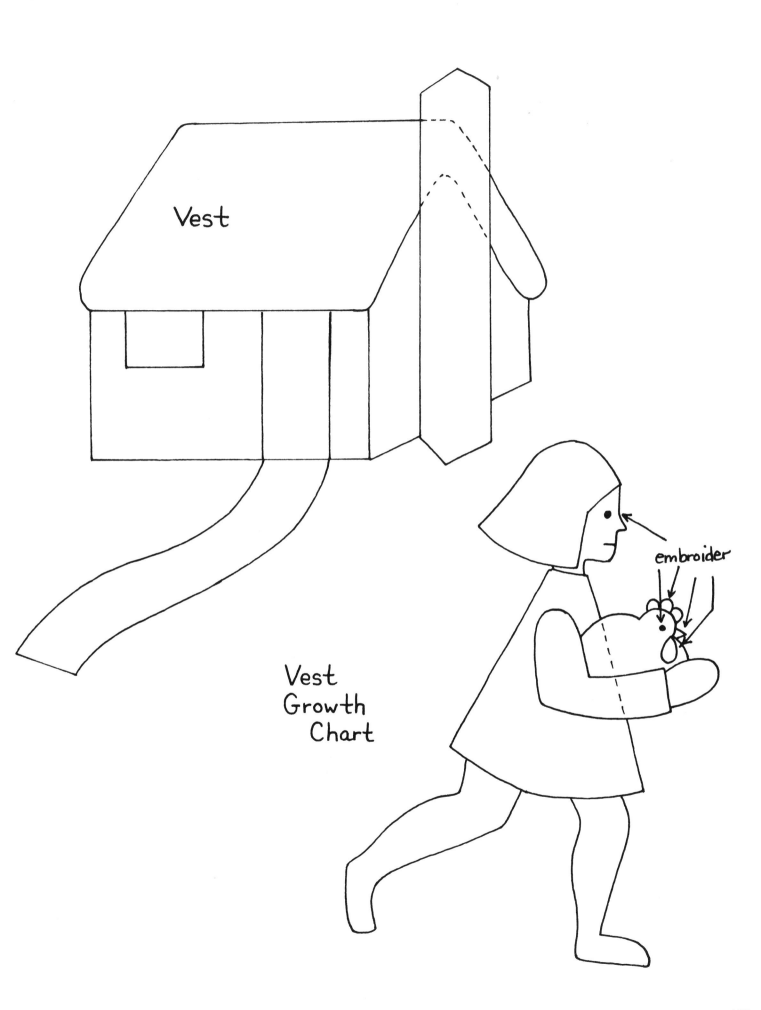

Vest

Vest
Growth
Chart

embroider

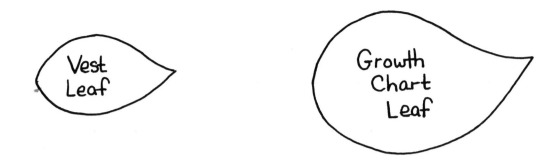

Vest
Leaf

Growth
Chart
Leaf

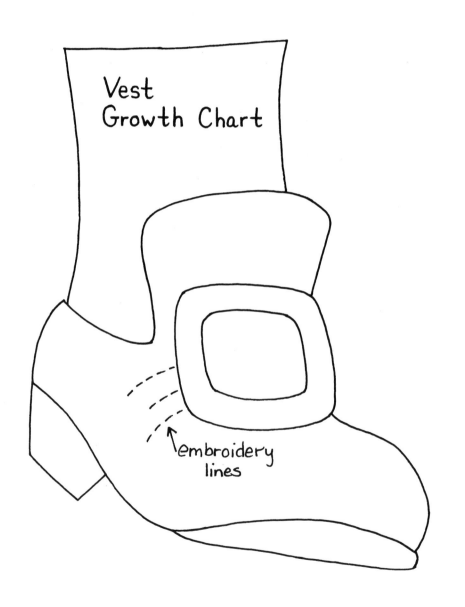

Vest
Growth Chart

embroidery
lines

"Bag of Gold"

coin

"BEANS" Bag

191

INDEX

Page numbers in *italics* refer to photographs, drawings, and patterns

193